The Case of the Nazi Professor

THE CASE OF THE NAZI PROFESSOR

David M. Oshinsky
Richard P. McCormick
Daniel Horn

Rutgers University Press
New Brunswick and London

Copyright © 1989 by Rutgers, The State University
All Rights Reserved
Manufactured in the United States of America

Library of Congress Cataloging-in-Publication Data

Oshinsky, David M.
  The case of the Nazi professor / David M. Oshinsky,
  Richard P. McCormick, Daniel Horn.
      p.   cm.
    Bibliography: p.
    Includes index.
    ISBN 0-8135-1363-4   ISBN 0-8135-1427-4 (pbk.)
    1. Academic freedom—New Jersey—History—20th century.
2. College teachers—New Jersey—Dismissal of—History—20th
century.   3. Bergel, Lienhard, 1905–1987.   4. Hauptmann, Friederich.
5. Politics and education—New Jersey—History—20th century.
6. Right and left (Political science)   7. Fascism—New Jersey—
History—20th century.   I. McCormick, Richard P. (Richard Patrick),
1916–   .   II. Horn, Daniel.   III. Title.
LC72.3.N5083   1989
378′.121—dc19   88-16895
                                          CIP

British Cataloging-in-Publication information available

All illustrations courtesy of Special Collections and Archives,
Rutgers University Libraries.

Contents

Acknowledgments   *vii*

1   Prologue   *1*

2   The Decision   *7*

3   The Decision Reaffirmed   *22*

4   Rumors   *30*

5   The Crisis   *44*

6   The Hearings   *57*

7   The Aftermath   *75*

8   The Cover-Up   *88*

9   Working for the Nazis   *98*

Epilogue   *108*

Summary of Findings   *113*

Notes   *121*

A Note about the Sources   *149*

Index   *153*

Illustrations appear between pages 43 and 44.

Acknowledgments

We would like to acknowledge the enormous assistance we received in the researching and writing of this book. Our first—and primary—debt is to Rutgers University Archivist Ruth Simmons and her staff. Under Ruth's supervision, the Department of Special Collections expertly compiled and categorized much of the primary material we used for this project. We must also thank the staff of the Seeley-Mudd Library, Princeton University, for locating and photocopying relevant portions of the Papers of the American Civil Liberties Union; and the archivists at the headquarters of the American Association of University Professors, Washington, D.C., for sending us AAUP documents relating to the Bergel-Hauptmann case.

Many others helped along the way. We are indebted to our colleague Harold Poor for obtaining valuable documents at the German Federal Archives in Koblenz. We are grateful to Erna K. Neuse of the Rutgers German Department for providing information about Professor Max Deutschbein, who directed Hauptmann's dissertation at the University of Marburg. And we owe thanks to Professor Fritz Fellner of the University of Salzburg and his assistants Johann Kolmbauer and Michael Mooslechner for the important material they supplied about Hauptmann's life in post–World War II Austria.

We are also grateful to those who provided information to us through oral interviews and written communications. They include: Lienhard Bergel, Sylvia Bergel, Evalyn Clark, Margaret Dahm, Mary Hartman, Emil Jordan, Alice Y. Kaplan, Martha Leonard, Albert Meder, Edna Newby, Alan Silver, Marion Short Sauer, Marjorie Strickman, and Torun Willits.

Finally, we would like to thank Tilden Edelstein, Dean of the Faculty of Arts and Sciences, for providing the financial assistance necessary for this project, and Marilyn Campbell, managing editor of the Rutgers University Press, for carefully guiding our manuscript through the editorial process. We, the authors, have enjoyed complete freedom in our research and our writing; we, the authors, are jointly responsible for the findings.

The Case of the Nazi Professor

In the spring of 1935, a young instructor of German at Rutgers University charged that he had been fired because he disagreed with the pro-Nazi views of his department head. After a grueling public investigation, the instructor's charge was rejected, his dismissal upheld. In a matter of months, the incident faded from view. As one reporter noted that fall, "On the [Rutgers] campus, all is quiet. Undergraduates who threw themselves into the dispute with youthful zest last Spring feel . . . the matter is over." [1]

It did not turn out that way. Exactly fifty years later—on May 5, 1985—an article about the incident appeared in the *New Brunswick Home News*. Written by a reporter named Peter Parisi, it was a damning indictment of those responsible for the instructor's dismissal. Parisi got most of his information from a Rutgers alumnus named Alan Silver. He also interviewed the one-time instructor on the telephone.

The instructor's name was Lienhard Bergel, and the story he told Parisi was chilling indeed. Bergel had left his native Germany in 1931 to take a teaching position at the New Jersey College for Women (later Douglass College). Before long, however, he discovered that his colleagues in the German Department were Nazi supporters, and his department head, Friedrich J. Hauptmann, a Nazi official. Bergel claimed that Hauptmann had "read him a letter from Joseph Goebbels, Adolf Hitler's propaganda minister, [which] . . . appointed Hauptmann 'the leader of the Germans' in Central New Jersey." Bergel added that Hauptmann "expected him to distribute propaganda materials and take the first ten minutes of his classes to rebut 'lies' about the Nazi regime." When Bergel

refused to do these things, he was labeled incompetent and eventually fired.

Parisi then described the protests surrounding Bergel's dismissal. Students, alumni, and local citizens pressured the Rutgers administration to reverse its decision. In response, President
Robert C. Clothier appointed a committee of five prominent trustees to investigate the instructor's allegations. After hearing testimony by more than a hundred witnesses, the trustees issued a
forty-thousand-word report "clearing Hauptmann and approving
Bergel's dismissal." This decision was upheld by the full Board of
Trustees in October 1935.

In his interview with Parisi, Bergel said that an FBI agent had
approached him as the hearings ended. The agent not only portrayed Hauptmann as "the leader of a spy ring that observed U.S.
ship and troop movements" in the New York—New Jersey area,
but also recruited Bergel to work for the Bureau. "So on the day I
lost my job [at Rutgers]," Bergel recalled, "I had another job with
the FBI." In 1938 he accepted a teaching position at Queens College
in New York City, remaining there until his retirement in 1974.

There was more to the story. In 1940 "Hauptmann disappeared after borrowing $900 from a bank and arranging a medical
leave from N.J.C." He fled the United States, Parisi went on, "to
become part of the Nazi propaganda machine in Czechoslovakia."
Following World War II, a Rutgers alumnus named Edward Cap,
who worked for Army Intelligence in Europe, discovered Hauptmann's photograph in a pile of captured enemy documents. Cap
told a friend in New Brunswick that Hauptmann had been arrested
by the allies. When the news became public in 1946, President
Clothier was asked to reopen the case, but he refused to do so.

Parisi's story was picked up by other newspapers, which added
details of their own. *Newsday* described Hauptmann as "head of the
Bratislava branch of the Goebbels machine in Czechoslovakia until
1946, when he was captured in a 900-year-old castle . . . filled
with the records of thousands of Nazi agents around the world."
The *Toronto Globe and Mail* portrayed him as both "a Nazi spy
while . . . at Rutgers" and "a senior propagandist for Goebbels."
"Rutgers has never apologized for its shabby treatment of Prof.

Bergel," the piece continued. "His dismissal for incompetence is still on the records."[2]

These newspaper accounts were accompanied by some stinging editorials. Three days after Parisi's story appeared, the *Home News* said it was "time to correct an injustice." Since Bergel had been "dismissed on what history has shown to be trumped-up charges," the newspaper suggested a remedy. "Probably the most that Rutgers can do now is to clear the record with an apology for injustice by a previous administration. It is also the least that Rutgers can do." A month later, the *Home News* criticized the current Rutgers president, Edward J. Bloustein, for refusing to reopen the case. "The mists of time," it wrote, "are not so thick as to be impenetrable even after 50 years."[3]

In taking this position, the *Home News* echoed the views of Alan Silver, the person responsible for reviving interest in the Bergel-Hauptmann case. A resident of Highland Park, adjacent to New Brunswick, Silver headed his own firm of management consultants. As a senior at Rutgers in 1935, he had been one of Bergel's strongest supporters. Fifty years later, he told a reporter,

> the Bitburg controversy was heating up and then I read about an anti-apartheid demonstration at Rutgers aimed at getting the university to disinvest. The administration refused, and so I was reminded of other unethical actions at Rutgers. I realized it was the 50th anniversary of the Bergel case. I remembered how things were in 1935—everything was upside down on campus, like Alice in Wonderland or something. I decided 50 years was long enough, it was time to right a terrible wrong.[4]

Silver went to work. He read old newspaper files and searched the university archives. He contacted individuals who had direct knowledge of the affair—including Lienhard and Sylvia Bergel—and made his findings available to the press. He sent lengthy memos, with selected supporting documents, to an ever-widening network of correspondents. Before long, Silver was modestly comparing his cause to the Alfred Dreyfus case—and himself to Emile Zola! "The battle for decency," he noted, "never ends."[5]

Silver ran into some early resistance. His demand that Rutgers reopen the case was initially rejected. President Bloustein told the *Home News* that "the matter should be left to history." He added: "I cannot change what took place, and I have no basis on which to be sure whether the trustees five decades since treated Mr. Bergel unfairly."[6]

Silver was persistent. Writing to Bloustein in June, he called upon Rutgers to "rehabilitate" Bergel from the "trumped-up charges of incompetence leveled against him [in 1935] by Dr. Friedrich J. Hauptmann, the virulently pro-Nazi head of the German Department at New Jersey College for Women." Silver also included a seven-page summary of his own research, to give Bloustein "easy access to all the relevant facts of this case."[7]

Bloustein replied that there was "no rational way, fifty years later," to judge whether the Rutgers trustees had come to a correct conclusion in 1935. He then told Silver:

> I would like to leave the matter rest by saying that, if Professor Bergel's academic qualifications were indeed assessed with political bias by the avowed Nazi, Professor Hauptmann, as a result of the anti-Nazi views held by Professor Bergel, it was a shameful act, unworthy of this or any other university. But whether political bias was indeed the basis of the assessment is a fact better left for determination by trained historians than by a university president.[8]

Undeterred, Silver pressed his attack. He mailed clippings, documents, and correspondence to reporters, politicians, alumni, academics, and friends. He enlisted the support of the local chapter of the American Association of University Professors. And he wrote other letters to Bloustein, pointing out the unfavorable publicity that Rutgers was receiving, and implying that more was on the way. "I frankly find it hard to believe that a liberal like you," he declared, "doesn't personally believe that exonerating Bergel is the right thing to do."[9]

These tactics produced a partial victory. In August 1985 President Bloustein asked the Dean of the Faculty of Arts and Sciences, Dr. Tilden Edelstein, to appoint a panel of historians "to review the records of the Bergel case and to comment on it from their historical perspective." Rutgers promised to publish the findings of these historians, who were appointed the following month. Press reaction was highly favorable. The *New York Times*, the *Newark Star Ledger*, and the *Home News* all applauded Bloustein's "wise" decision. "The remedy he has chosen," said the *Times*, "employs the tools of the academician, scholarly inquiry, to achieve the closest thing to justice that is now possible: an exposition of the facts, carefully discerned and widely disseminated."[10]

No one was more surprised by the reopening of this case than the surviving central figure. Now eighty years old, Bergel lived in quiet retirement with his wife, Sylvia, in Port Washington, New York. He was affectionately remembered by his former colleagues at Queens College as a "Mr. Chips figure," an "old-world scholar and a gentleman." Bergel's first reaction was to dismiss as "immaterial" any apology by Rutgers officials. But then he changed his mind. In one of his numerous press interviews, he explained:

> I'm an old man. I don't need vindication. It would be nice to get an apology and have the word "incompetent" erased from my record. But no one at Rutgers or anywhere else can subtract from my life's work. They can't do me any harm. I have reflected on this a long time. This is important for the members of my profession—that we be allowed to speak and to stand up for our beliefs even if we disagree with an administration that is immoral. It is Rutgers that needs vindication. They have dirty linen to air. They have a chance to take another look at this Hauptmann fellow and do the right thing.[11]

Sylvia Bergel took a less dispassionate view. Writing to President Bloustein, she noted that her husband's academic credentials were far superior to Hauptmann's, and that Hitler's statements in 1935 left no doubt about his plans for Germany or his solution to the "Jewish problem." "Yet when Mr. Bergel revealed the Nazi propaganda activities in the classrooms of N.J.C., as carried on by F. J. Hauptmann and his colleagues, the Trustees, instead of cleaning up the nest of Nazis, stigmatized Mr. Bergel as 'incompetent,' and 'intolerant.'" Even worse, when Hauptmann fled to Germany in 1940, Rutgers administrators "did nothing to retract their support of Hauptmann or the charge of incompetence against Lienhard Bergel."[12]

It was against this background that our committee was created. We have tried to produce a full account of the Bergel-Hauptmann affair. In the course of our investigation, we have addressed many question. Why was Bergel's appointment terminated? Was he ever charged with "incompetence"? Was he fired for political reasons? Why did the case arouse so much interest and controversy? How extensive was the hearing in 1935 by a committee of trustees? How fairly was it conducted? How valid were the committee's findings? Was Hauptmann a Nazi spy and later a functionary in Goebbel's propaganda machine in Czechoslovakia? How reliable were the press stories in 1985 that led to the reopening of the case? While pursuing the answers, we have been led, inevitably, to raise a number of additional questions, ranging from the nature of the American Nazi movement in the 1930s to the precise details of personnel policies at Rutgers in that era. For us, the endeavor has been extremely challenging and thoroughly absorbing. We can only hope that our readers experience the same feelings. In the end, of course, they will form their own conclusions.

2 THE DECISION

Rutgers University in 1932—when Lienhard Bergel joined the faculty—was a relatively small institution with fewer than three thousand full-time undergraduates. Founded in 1766, Rutgers had close ties to the Dutch Reformed Church during its first century. With its designation as a land-grant college in 1864, it acquired an ill-defined relationship to the State of New Jersey. The legislature began to make annual appropriations to the institution early in the twentieth century—rising to a level of more than a million dollars by 1930—but Rutgers did not have the status of a state university. Instead, it was managed by a "private" Board of Trustees on which state appointees were a minority.[1]

In an effort to clarify the relationship of Rutgers to the state, the legislature created a Board of Regents in 1929. This agency was charged with determining the needs of New Jersey in the area of public higher education. Each year the Regents contracted with Rutgers for educational services, but precise funding depended on legislative action. Rutgers' private resources were modest, for, with an endowment of only $4 million and an outstanding debt of more than a million, its financial condition was precarious. Even worse, it felt threatened by sporadic campaigns to establish a "free state university," and by frequent claims that New Jersey should not contribute funds to a "private" institution.

The main undergraduate units of the University in New Brunswick were the so-called "men's colleges"—Arts and Sciences, Agriculture, Engineering, and Education—and the New Jersey College for Women. There also were divisions offering extension programs for several thousand part-time students. Graduate studies, carried on mainly at the College of Agriculture, were under the jurisdiction of the Graduate Faculty, organized in 1932.

Personnel policies at Rutgers could best be described as traditional and rudimentary. The University had not yet acted to comply with the guidelines recommended by the American Association of University Professors. Faculty self-governance, aside from purely curricular matters, was negligible. The responsibility for managing each department was vested in a "head," who was chosen by the appropriate dean. No faculty committees were involved in the appointment, promotion, or dismissal of faculty members. There were no formal provisions for tenure, although those above the rank of instructor, barring serious budget cuts or manifestly unsatisfactory performance, could assume security in their jobs. There were no grievance procedures beyond a personal appeal to a dean, the President, or, in rare cases, the Board of Trustees.[2]

The Great Depression brought hard times to Rutgers. The state appropriation for 1932–1933 was slashed by 20 percent, forcing a 10-percent salary cut and a severe reduction in staff. Another budget cut the following year brought a 5-percent drop in salaries. The legislature had also mandated that there could be no pay increases from state funds, a policy that was to remain in effect for several years. By 1935–1936 a modest rise in the state appropriation made possible a partial restoration of the earlier pay cuts, but not until 1937–1938 was the state's contribution to the university's budget brought up to the pre-1932 level. Unable to make salary increases, the University all but halted promotions. By 1935 base salaries ranged from $1,620 for an instructor to $3,150 for a full professor.[3]

These problems were compounded by declining enrollments. The number of male undergraduates dropped from 1,401 in 1929 to 1,195 in 1934, before beginning a slow climb upward. There was a similar loss at the New Jersey College for Women during this period—from 1,159 to 917—and recovery in enrollments did not match that of the men's colleges. Moreover, as undergraduates became concerned with their employment prospects, they moved toward vocationally oriented subjects. Thus, the humanities suffered most of all.[4]

The New Jersey College for Women—where Bergel worked—was created by the trustees in 1918 as a "department" of the University. Located about a mile from the main campus, on the other side of New Brunswick, it had grown rapidly under the leadership of Dean Mabel Smith Douglass. By 1928, N.J.C. produced more graduates than the men's colleges. Three years later, it was placed on the accepted list of the Association of American Universities.

One of the top priorities of Dean Douglass was to build her own faculty. Until 1927 the College had been staffed mainly by teachers from the men's colleges; by 1930, however, all but 14 of the 102 instructors at N.J.C. taught there exclusively. Without seeking the approval of the Board of Trustees, the Dean also proceeded to organize her faculty into departments distinct from those of the men's colleges. The peculiar status of N.J.C. aroused the concern of the Board of Regents, which insisted that the College be brought under the control of the trustees. As a result, the university's charter was amended in 1932 to provide for the election of five women trustees to a ten-member "Trustees Committee on the College for Women." At the same time, Dean Douglass was ordered to submit her annual budget to the President for the approval of the trustees. These actions were significant; they served to integrate the Women's College with the other units of the University.[5]

When Dean Douglass organized the N.J.C. German Department in 1928, she chose Friedrich Hauptmann as acting chairman (or head). Hauptmann had been born in Saxony, Germany, in 1890, and had grown up in modest surroundings. The son of a railway clerk, he attended a secondary school (*Realgymnasium*) that emphasized vocational pursuits. After graduating he spent several unhappy years "in business," apparently as a salesman, before entering the German Army during World War I. Beginning as a common soldier, he rose to the rank of deputy sergeant major, an event of great significance in his life. The Prussian-dominated army was known for its class consciousness, its iron discipline, and its rigid chain of command. Non-commissioned officers were supposed to treat subordinates harshly, and superiors with craven respect. A deputy sergeant major expressed his authority by shouting insults and commands. He expected immediate and absolute compliance from his troops; the process was known as *Kadavergehorsam*, "the obedience of corpses." There is strong evidence—as we shall see—that Hauptmann continued this behavior for the rest of his life.[6]

Like many veterans, Hauptmann was shattered by Germany's final defeat in 1918. Having shared the illusion of victory for so long, he could not easily accept the "humiliation" his country had suffered at Versailles. Determined now to be a teacher, he drifted from one university to another before settling at Marburg in 1921. The choice does not seem accidental. Marburg had many students like Hauptmann. It was a hotbed of right-radical politics, a center for those who feared the changes and reforms that swept Germany after World War I.[7]

Hauptmann apparently passed the state examination for teachers of higher schools (the *Staatsexamen*) in 1922. He had hoped to obtain a position teaching theology, but his plans did not materialize. After working for several months at a middle school in Dresden, he decided to leave Germany. His decision almost certainly was based on his bleak job prospects and his disdain for the new German Democratic state. In 1923 Hauptmann and his wife Anna Marie sailed for the United States.

Their first year in America was a difficult one. Hauptmann drifted from job to job. He worked as a laborer in Rochester, New York, and as an assistant Lutheran pastor in Manhattan. In 1924 he got a break; he was hired as an instructor of German at Gettysburg College in Pennsylvania. The appointment was apparently for five years, but he left in 1927 because of charges involving the neglect of a German foster child in his care. Although he maintained that the charges were "a mistake," he "felt he ought not remain at the college."[8]

Hauptmann arrived in New Brunswick a few months later. Beginning as an instructor at the Women's College, he became an associate professor and permanent department head in 1931. Under his aggressive leadership, the number of full-year German courses rose from five in 1928 to twelve in 1932, and student enrollment increased from 113 to 284. Hauptmann's staff at N.J.C. included

Dr. Emil Jordan, a trained economist with an interest in German cultural geography; Alice Schlimbach, who directed the campus German House in addition to her teaching responsibilities; and Marie Hauptmann—the chairman's wife—who taught part-time and bore the title of assistant. All were German-born and educated in line with the college policy of having the modern languages taught by native speakers.[9]

The University at this time did not encourage serious scholarship on the part of its faculty. The emphasis was on undergraduate education. That philosophy embraced not only classroom instruction but also the whole social and moral environment that constituted the college community. As the Rutgers president explained in 1933: "Education, which means the development of the student's *whole personality* rather than his intellect alone, is achieved, not solely out of books nor in lectures, but in personal association with gifted men and women who are themselves the kind of people we want these young persons to become."[10] Faculty members, then, were expected to be exemplary role models and to work closely with students inside and outside the classroom.

The German program at N.J.C. reflected this philosophy. The classroom emphasis was on acquiring competence in the written and spoken language (along with exposure in advanced courses to the treasures of German literature and culture). There were supplements to the formal instruction, however, including the German House, the German Club, and the German table in the dining hall. It was assumed that members of the department would take part in these extra-curricular activities, all of which were well established by 1932.[11]

Lienhard Bergel's appointment to the N.J.C. faculty resulted from unusual circumstances. When the academic year began in September 1931 the newest member of the German Department was Erna Zoller. She had come from Germany as an exchange instructor, but problems soon developed. Hauptmann claimed that she was both a Communist and an advocate of companionate marriage. These charges may have been true; it is also true that Zoller resented—and openly challenged—the authoritarian manner in which Hauptmann dealt with his subordinates. On one occasion, she told the startled chairman that "he could yell at his wife, he could yell at the students, he could yell at his children, but he couldn't yell at her." Miss Zoller did not last the term.[12]

She was replaced by Sylvia Cook, an honor graduate of Barnard College who had just returned from two years of study in Germany. Miss Cook was engaged to a young scholar she had met in Breslau, Lienhard Bergel, who wanted to join her in the United States.

Bergel was born in Silesia, Germany, in 1905. His middle-class family included several generations of Lutheran ministers. After graduating with distinction from a classical *Gymnasium*, he had studied at universities in Munich and Vienna, and for five years at the University of Breslau. His major fields were Germanic and Romance philology, but his real interest was comparative literature. He had passed the *Staatsexamen* in 1930.

Bergel got his job at N.J.C. by replacing Miss Cook, who had lobbied for the switch since her arrival in New Brunswick. He came with superb recommendations from his mentor at Breslau and from Professor William A. Braun of Barnard College. Appointed an instructor in February 1932, Bergel married Miss Cook a short time later. His salary was $1,800 a year.[13]

Even before his arrival, Bergel had been "warned" by Miss Cook about what she regarded as undesirable conditions in the German Department. When compared with its counterpart at Barnard, she felt that the N.C.J. department left much to be desired, both in leadership and scholarly credentials. Despite these danger signals, Bergel recalled, he accepted the position and tried to keep an open mind. During his first semester, he taught a full schedule of elementary and advanced courses and worked to improve his limited command of English. There were some criticisms of his teaching at this time, but when Hauptmann told Bergel about them, his intervention was resented. Still, the young instructor was routinely reappointed for the academic year 1932–1933.[14]

Bergel and Hauptmann had almost nothing in common. Bergel had been too young to fight in World War I. He did not look back nostalgically to the great days of the German Empire, and he strongly opposed the rise of Adolf Hitler. Politically, the two men were worlds apart—yet politics did not tell the whole story. Bergel and Hauptmann came from different backgrounds, different generations, different ways of life. Bergel called himself a "bookworm." Belonging to the *Bildungsbuergertum,* or educated middle class, he seemed quite conscious of his superior intellect and training, and quite ready to flaunt them. It was no secret, for example, that the Bergels considered the Hauptmanns their social and intellectual inferiors. Indeed, the Bergels once described Friedrich Hauptmann as a "soap and perfume salesman," and his wife Marie as a "former governess."

Opinions about Bergel differed widely at N.J.C. His liberal views and obvious intelligence won him many admirers among the students and faculty. In the eyes of his department colleagues, however, he was a rather stiff and arrogant young man who looked down upon the qualifications of others. His commitment to the German academic tradition seemed out of place in New Brunswick—and more than a trifle extreme.

On January 20, 1933, Adolf Hitler became the German Chancellor. The American press during the next few months reported such sensational events as the Reichstag fire, the Nazi attempts to suppress political opposition, the heated campaign that preceded the March 5 election, Hitler's dubious triumph with only 44 percent of the total vote, and the adoption of the so-called Enabling Act, which conferred dictatorial powers on the Chancellor. There also were vivid accounts of the terror created by Nazi stormtroopers, and the one-day boycott of all Jewish business, organized by Julius Streicher.

Most American were too busy with the problems of the Depression to think much about foreign events. For certain groups, however, the coming of Hitler could hardly be ignored. To a segment of the large German-American population, the fall of the Weimar Republic and the rise of a charismatic *Fuehrer* who promised to restore the Reich to its former grandeur were welcome events. Ardent support for the new regime was expressed most blatantly in the U.S. by the Friends of the New Germany, which paraded with swastika, spread Nazi propaganda in its publications, and received covert funding from German sources until about 1935.[15]

Not surprisingly, the strongest opposition to Hitler's regime came from Jewish organizations. In April 1933 the American Jewish Congress and B'nai B'rith called for a boycott of German-made products, although the American Jewish Committee favored a more cautious approach in confronting Nazism. After the excesses of the first few months, as Hitler sought to consolidate his position, there were fewer sensational reports from Germany, but the activities of American Nazis, especially in the New York region, were frequently in the headlines.[16]

At Rutgers, as in the nation at large, there was little interest in German affairs until after Hitler came to power. Student groups such as the Liberal Club, the Student's Forum, and the League of Women Voters discussed economic and social problems and the broad issue of maintaining peace. Interviewed by the *Campus News*, the N.J.C. student newspaper, in February 1932, Lienhard Bergel spoke mainly of the differences between the German and American educational systems, but he did note that economic conditions in Germany were very bad and that there was considerable political unrest. In April a Columbia professor spoke to the N.J.C. History Club on "The Hitler Movement: Its Domestic and Foreign Implications." In a rather bland presentation, she observed that the movement stood for "all that the new generation desires." A N.J.C. student who had spent her junior year in Germany reported her experiences to *Campus News*. While in Berlin, she had witnessed a student riot that pitted Hitlerites against Social Democrats. "There is nothing vicious about these outbursts, despite what newspapers say about them," she said. In December 1932 Professor Albert Holzmann of the Rutgers German Department told the Students' Forum that conditions in Germany were "pitiful." The German people, he asserted, "had republicanism thrust upon them by the allies when they were unfit for the responsibility of self-government." Holzmann predicted that the nation would turn in desperation to Communism or to the reestablishment of the monarchy.[17]

Late in March 1933, with Hitler's ascendance now a reality, the campus was aroused—though briefly—by a discussion of the political upheaval in Germany. On March 29 Dr. Emil Jordan of the N.J.C. German Department spoke to the campus League of Women Voters on "Hitlerism." The Nazi movement, he argued, was "the logical continuation of . . . conditions in the nineteenth century which have brought about the unification of Germany." He was, he said, not personally trying to defend Hitler but to present him as the German people saw him. "Fourteen years of the Republic left Germany worse off than ever," he observed. Likening Hitler's policies to Roosevelt's New Deal, Jordan saw in both an effort to meet national emergencies. "When the present wave of excitement has died down, America will realize that she has much more in common with Germany than ever before. . . . Things are not as bad as the [American] press sees them." [18]

In the discussion that followed, Bergel challenged Jordan's interpretation of events in Germany from his own perspective as a Social Democrat. Despite the interchange, the two men left the meeting together on cordial terms. The next day, Bergel recalled, he was severely criticized by Hauptmann for taking such a strong public position against a colleague. According to Bergel, this incident marked the end of his social relations with the chairman and his wife. [19]

That same evening, a symposium on "Hitler: The German Scene," sponsored by the Rutgers Liberal Club, drew more than two hundred people. Professor Edward M. Burns of the history department led off with a denunciation of Nazism, but he acknowledged that, because of the injustices of the Versailles Treaty, Germany could not be blamed for the course it had taken. The next speaker, Professor Holzmann, tried to defend the Hitler regime against the charges of anti-Semitism. After deploring the "propaganda of atrocities which would smirch the fair name of the German people," he urged Americans to withhold judgment until they were provided with unbiased accounts of what was happening in Germany. [20]

Rabbi Nathaniel Keller of New Brunswick took issue with

Holzmann. Conceding that stories of atrocities were greatly exaggerated, he still insisted that there was considerable discrimination against Jews, and he called for public protests against the "misguided actions" of the German people. Taking the middle ground, Dr. Milton J. Hoffman of the New Brunswick Theological Seminary—known as a liberal and an anti-war activist—deplored "intolerance" but opposed the kind of protest favored by Rabbi Keller pending a thorough investigation of the facts. "When things have quieted down," he concluded, "we will probably find that some sporadic outrages have been committed, but not the foul stories which we are hearing now."

Professor Hauptmann took part in the audience discussion. He tried to mitigate the charges of anti-Semitism by noting that Germans had no quarrel with Jewish families who had been in the country for several generations. There was only opposition to the Jews who had migrated from Poland after 1918. These recent immigrants, he said, had strengthened the ranks of the Socialists and Communists and had brought overcrowding to such urban centers as Berlin. Like Holzmann and Hoffman, he made a plea against hasty judgments and asked for understanding of the German point of view.[21]

The symposium received mixed reviews. The reporter for the *Daily Home News* was not impressed. The "whole issue," he wrote, was "as clouded [at the end of the evening] as at the outset." But an editorial in *Targum,* the Rutgers student newspaper, hailed the symposium and its "eminently qualified speakers." Their remarks, it said, "gave full evidence . . . that there is always more than one side and that dogmatic support of one, without due consideration of the other, is never . . . justified."[22]

These neutral observations probably represented the dominant viewpoint on campus at this time. Most people seemed uninterested, or unwilling to take a stand. Among the exceptions was Dr. Jacob G. Lipman, Dean of the College of Agriculture. In an interview with the *Daily Home News,* he said that the Jews in Germany were being used as scapegoats for the country's post-war problems. "There must be two Germanies," he suggested. "There [are] the kindly, honest people whom we all know and admire, and there are those who bear a streak of cruelty and meanness such as the present regime displays."[23]

The newspaper also interviewed Professor Hauptmann. He took a more positive approach, describing Germany as a cultured, well-meaning nation in the midst of a revolutionary crisis. His plea was to "let Germany alone. Give them time." He was asked whether Hitler had the qualities of a leader. "Of an agitator, yes," he responded. "Of a leader—we must wait. He has given us many words. Now we must see some deeds. To judge Hitler as a leader will take time."[24]

Campus interest in the Hitler phenomenon quickly dwindled. Students were more concerned about jobs, the peace movement, and the New Deal, along with more frivolous matters. But Professor Holzmann—not Hauptmann—continued to be in demand as a commentator on developments in Germany. A native of Newark, he had graduated from Rutgers with Phi Beta Kappa honors in 1917, served in the U.S. Army for three years, taught in local high schools, and joined the Rutgers faculty in 1923. He remained there until his retirement in 1960, serving as head of his department for twenty-six years. In talks to various groups in New Jersey, Holzmann offered a sympathetic interpretation of the Nazi regime. Hitler, he told one gathering, had "realized the dream of Bismarck" in unifying the German people. Moreover, "in his exclusion of the Jews from economic life, [he] had seized upon a sore spot in the side of the German people and used it as an effective political weapon." Holzmann declared himself to be "eighty-five percent in approval of Hitler and the Nazi regime"—a statement that aroused a few Jewish leaders in New Brunswick, but almost no one else.[25]

For university officials, the politics of Germany seemed confusing and remote. There were more pressing matters to consider, brought on by reductions in state funding and student enrollments. Salaries had been cut, promotions had been deferred, the staff had been reduced. With the Depression in full swing, there was every reason to anticipate continued austerity. In response, the trustees adopted a new policy that would have a telling impact upon Lienhard Bergel's future at Rutgers.

Prior to 1933, there was no fixed limit on the number of years one might serve in the rank of instructor. Nor, for that matter, were there any guidelines to evaluate instructors for promotion in rank. On February 24, 1933, the Board of Trustees took the following step:

> On recommendation of the President it was voted to approve in principle a new regulation by which Instructors in the University shall be appointed annually with this rank for a period not exceeding three years, except that at the discretion of the Dean of the College concerned it may be extended one additional year making it four years in all.[26]

This was known as the "three-year rule." It meant that if an instructor was not deemed eligible for promotion to assistant professor within three years, his or her job would ordinarily be terminated. An instructorship was now viewed as a probationary appointment; some would advance, others would not. For those already at that rank, the three-year period would start on July 1, 1932.

The trustees did not say anything about promotion standards. So Albert E. Meder, the acting dean at N.J.C., formulated his own criteria. He said that every instructor who desired promotion should ask himself the following questions:

(1) Is my teaching ability unusually outstanding?
(2) Have I contributed to the advancement of scholarship in my field through research, publication, or the like?
(3) Is my general usefulness to the institution better than average, and do I bring prestige to the institution?[27]

To these stated criteria, a proviso was added. Because it was the general policy not to give promotions unless they were accompanied by appropriate salary increases, budgetary considerations could be a limiting factor. If sufficient funds were not available, promotions would have to be denied, or deferred.

In the spring of 1933 Dean Meder met with Hauptmann to discuss personnel arrangements in the German Department. According to Meder's account, prepared in 1935, the three-year rule was discussed at some length. There were two instructors in the department, Jordan and Bergel. How, asked Meder, would the three-year rule affect their prospects? Hauptmann replied "that Mr. Jordan should be slated for promotion when possible and that Mr. Bergel should not." To support his case, Hauptmann said that Jordan was a good teacher, a mature colleague, and a promising scholar who would soon be publishing a book. Such positive indicators were lacking in Bergel's case; on the contrary, there were "valid reasons why he should not be promoted." [28]

What were they? "A decrease in enrollments was anticipated, and Mr. Bergel was the junior appointee." Some doubts had been cast on Bergel's teaching effectiveness, and there were complaints from students. Members of his class in beginning German had not performed well on a uniform test and their grades seemed inflated. On a personal level, Bergel was not "the sort of man . . . we wished to have," and his wife did not fit in, either. Finally, Bergel gave "no evidence of possessing interests which would contribute to his general academic usefulness." These allegations, in one form or another, were to be subjects of future controversy. At the close of this fateful conference, Hauptmann was advised to tell Bergel to "look actively for another position."

Hauptmann did not immediately communicate this news to Bergel. Indeed, a few weeks later, on June 24, Bergel received his letter of reappointment for the next academic year. Mrs. Bergel was relieved. She wrote in her notebook: "Definite notice that Lienhard's job O.K. for next year from Pres. Clothier." During that summer, Bergel spoke with Hauptmann about the possibility of securing a leave of absence for research at some time in the future. He had no inkling that a decision had already been made to dismiss him. [29]

The bad news came in September. Hauptmann told Bergel about his conference with Meder—and the decision to choose Jordan alone for promotion. He added that Bergel should begin looking for other jobs, although, under the three-year rule, he could expect a final reappointment for the academic year 1934–1935. When Bergel asked for an explanation, Hauptmann said "he wanted a change; 'fresh blood' in his department." He did not go further than that. [30]

Bergel wanted more. He went to see Dean Meder, who

informed him about the three-year rule, said nothing critical of his work, but reaffirmed the decision that had been made. According to Meder, Bergel did not try to portray himself as a victim of political discrimination; the issue never came up. Bergel was more interested in learning whether his scheduled termination was due to any deficiencies on his part. Meder said he knew of none—which was untrue—but that he would "let him know if there were any new developments." Bergel did not hear from Meder again. The acting dean returned to his post in the Mathematics Department three months later.[31]

Meanwhile, Bergel contacted Professor William A. Braun of the Barnard College German Department—the man who had recommended him for the N.J.C. position and with whom Mrs. Bergel had studied as an undergraduate. Braun wrote to Meder about Bergel's situation; the young man, he said, had "some misgivings as to the security of his position." Meder responded promptly. He explained the three-year rule and the financial problems at N.J.C. He then went to the heart of the matter:

> For budgetary reasons, there seems to be no prospect of the creation of an additional assistant professorship in the Department of German in the near future. Even if this were possible it is improbable that Mr. Bergel, as the junior member of the Department, would receive the appointment. For this reason, it was felt to be a protection to him to inform him of the situation, and to suggest that he begin actively to look for a place elsewhere. If he fails to find such a position, his instructorship will be renewed—the budget permitting—until June 30, 1935.[32]

Had the full text of this letter been transmitted to Bergel, some of the later misunderstandings might have been avoided. Instead, Braun apparently told Mrs. Bergel that her husband did not have to worry about his job "for the next year." What interpretation Bergel placed upon this vague message is unclear. He probably assumed that his job was not in jeopardy. Indeed, he later remarked that he did not take the verbal notices from Hauptmann and Meder "very seriously," and thus made no real effort to find another post.[33]

What rankled Bergel was that—in his view—he had been given no "reasons" for his scheduled termination. Obviously, he did not accept the explanation that the three-year rule, the preference for Jordan, and the unfavorable budgetary outlook meant that there was no opportunity for him to remain beyond June 30, 1935. It was his deeply held conviction, derived largely from his experience in the German academic world, "that a teacher, if he is not retained, should get a reasonable explanation why he is not, and that he should have, if there is a charge against him, . . . a chance at least to defend himself." In his case, there had been no "charges." Why, then was he being dismissed? What was going on? [34]

Meder saw no need to answer these questions. The academic guidelines of that era did not require that an instructor on annual appointment be given reasons for his termination. According to the policies of the American Association of University Professors, an instructor could be discharged "by the mere act of giving a timely notice . . . to terminate." And Bergel had received nearly two years' verbal notice by Hauptmann and Meder that his appointment would not be renewed after June 30, 1935. Under ordinary circumstances, the whole matter would have ended here. What followed, however, could hardly be described as ordinary. [35]

3 THE DECISION REAFFIRMED

BY October 1933 Lienhard Bergel had little reason to antici-pate a long association with N.J.C. He had been told by the head of his department and by the acting dean of the college that he could not expect to retain his post as instructor beyond June 30, 1935. He had not been informed of any shortcomings on his part, although such matters had been discussed in the conference be-tween Professor Hauptmann and Dean Meder. His termination had been explained to him in rather general terms: the need for "new blood," the recent three-year rule for instructors, and the decision to choose Emil Jordan alone for promotion. Whatever his under-standing of the situation, Bergel was not disposed to accept the judgment that had been made. His academic qualifications, he be-lieved, were vastly superior to those of his colleagues, and he had confidence in his teaching ability. No charges had been brought against him. It all seemed so confusing and unfair.

During the academic year 1933–1934, conditions within the University worsened. The legislature imposed a second straight cut in the annual appropriation. The enrollment trend continued down-ward. Twenty-four faculty members were "released." President Clothier advised deans to prepare for a financial emergency. At N.J.C. the size of the entering freshman class fell from 341 to 277. There was a vacancy rate of 42 percent in the dormitories. Bergel's salary was reduced from $1,800 to $1,620, and others were simi-larly affected. The impact of the Depression was everywhere.[1]

At this critical juncture, the Women's College acquired a new dean, Margaret Trumbull Corwin. The daughter of a prominent

Yale professor, Miss Corwin had attended Bryn Mawr and served since 1919 as executive secretary of the Yale University Graduate School. Her academic experience was wholly administrative; she held no advanced degrees and had never taught. A diligent administrator, who lacked the flamboyant style of Mabel Smith Douglass, she brought order and stability to the College and developed a close working relationship with President Clothier. While Corwin championed the interests of N.J.C., she clearly recognized its place within the larger structure of Rutgers University. She would remain at the College for twenty-one years.[2]

The mood of the campus at this time was also undergoing important changes. Most conspicuous were the signs of increased student activism—and a movement to the left. In October 1932 a student poll at N.J.C. had shown that the overwhelming majority favored the reelection of President Herbert Hoover. By 1934 a clear majority of seniors identified themselves as Socialists, with Republicans taking second place, and Democrats running a distant third. Left-wing campus groups were now attracting provocative speakers like Norman Thomas, Earl Browder, and Scott Nearing. "When a Communist [Browder] spoke last week," said *Targum*, "Geological Hall could not hold all of the people who wished to hear the talk." The key issue on campus was peace—or rather the opposition to war and to American militarism in all its guises.[3]

The event that signaled the new initiative was a symposium organized in March 1934 by the Liberal Club and the N.J.C. League of Women Voters. Three hundred people filled the men's college chapel to hear several professors and students denounce war and military training. At about the same time, petitions were circulated urging the United States to take an official part in the deliberations of the League of Nations. *Targum* took a dim view of these activities. "There has been altogether too much agitation," it grumbled, "for ill-advised disarmament and peace moves on the part of professors and students here and elsewhere." Naturally, the president of the Liberal Club condemned this "vicious blow directed against the student movement in opposition to war which is emerging in all the universities in the country."[4]

Targum was probably unaware of the source of this emerging student peace movement. The chief sponsors were the Communist-led National Student League (NSL) and the Students' League for Industrial Democracy (SLID), a Socialist organization. In 1934 NSL and SLID cooperated in promoting a nation-wide student "Strike for Peace," to be held on April 13, the date of America's entry into World War I. Because of the popularity of the issue, other campus groups, including the Y.M.C.A., flocked to the cause. By April 1935 an estimated 150,000 students across the country had participated in the strike movement. Rutgers students were slow to move with the tide. There was no campus peace strike on April 13, 1934. But one did occur the following year, and it would have a real bearing on the affairs of Lienhard Bergel.[5]

Oddly, however, these political concerns did not initially include events in Hitler's Third Reich. There were occasional reports in the campus newspapers about the views of professors and students returning from Germany, but they aroused little comment. Professor Willem Rudolfs of the College of Agriculture was interviewed after a two-month tour. "The German people as a mass are solidly for the new regime," he said. "They feel that Adolf Hitler has brought unity to Germany and saved her from Communism." Edward Cap, a recent graduate who returned from a stay in Jena, was struck by the tranquillity there. Almost no one had a bad word for Hitler. Only Dr. Evalyn Clark of the N.J.C. Classics Department sounded a different note. In a talk to the League of Women Voters on "The Nazis in Germany," she deplored the uses of propaganda and terror to mold mass opinion. "There is a revolt against reason . . . ," she observed, "a wholesale negation of the nation's thinking."[6]

If events in Germany seemed remote, however, the antics of the pro-Nazi Friends of the New Germany (FONG) in the United States aroused some concern. In March 1934 the House of Representatives approved a resolution by Congressman Samuel Dickstein that called for the appointment of a committee to investigate Nazi subversion in the United States. The committee held hearings in major American cities and released alarming accounts of FONG activities. There were disclosures of financial aid from Germany, of para-military forces in stormtrooper uniforms, of bitterly anti-Semitic publications, and of youth camps where children were indoctrinated in Nazi ideology. Meanwhile, the newspapers reported frequent brawls in New York and New Jersey between men flaunting the swastika emblem and their outraged adversaries.

German-Americans who did not support the extremist views of FONG, but who nevertheless favored the "rebirth" of the fatherland, occupied an awkward position. Many of them recalled the hatred and abuse to which they had been subjected in the World War I era, when German language teaching, German music, and even German food had been all but banned. They now drew protectively together to avert a similar catastrophe. Mainstream German-American organizations like the Steuben Society and the Carl Schurz Memorial Foundation, as well as the leading German-language newspaper in New York City—the *Staatszeitung*—all refrained from criticizing the Hitler regime. At the same time, they sought to keep alive a strong regard for their ethnic heritage and to ward off anti-German discrimination.[7]

The problems of the Depression, the arrival of Dean Corwin, the rise of student activism, the growing concern with Hitler and his American supporters—all would play a role in the Bergel case. Taken together, they were to rivet national attention on a fragmented university and an obscure instructor of German. But that development was still several months away.

By September 1934 Lienhard Bergel had an uncomfortable role in both the German Department and the College itself. His relationship with Hauptmann was not cordial. He had been deprived of all advanced courses and taught only at the elementary and intermediate levels. By his own admission, he took little or no part in the activities of the German House and the German Club. He felt that his presence was not welcome, and he had a low opinion of these extracurricular activities. Furthermore, he almost never attended the meetings of the College faculty, which was very unusual at this time.

Beyond teaching his classes, Bergel spent little time on the campus. His activities outside the classroom were limited to occasional meetings of the French Club and the League of Women Voters. Much to his annoyance, he claimed, he was frequently engaged by Hauptmann in political discussions about Germany. In November 1933, when Hauptmann was ill, Bergel assumed part of his teaching load, and that spring, when Bergel was hospitalized with appendicitis, his classes were taught by Hauptmann and Jordan.

Bergel also refused to accept his verbal notices of dismissal. Upon returning to N.J.C. after his illness, he was asked by Professor Hauptmann about his search for other employment. To Hauptmann's amazement, Bergel replied that he did not expect to leave N.J.C. He had been assured by "high officials," he said, that his job was not in danger. According to Bergel, he again asked Hauptmann for the reasons behind his termination; the chairman said simply that "he did not want so many assistant professors in the department." Hauptmann, he added, made no complaints about his work but did say that if he had known that Bergel would be unwilling to change his opinion of Hitler, he never would have hired him.[9]

Hauptmann reported the conversation to Meder. Was it true, he asked, that "high officials" were protecting Bergel's job? Meder said no, it was not true. He advised Hauptmann to bring the matter to Dean Corwin's attention. Meanwhile, Meder spoke with Corwin and told her that "Mr. Bergel did not seem inclined to accept the situation."[10]

The Dean reviewed Bergel's status. She knew that the three-year rule applied here—that Bergel's appointment would normally be terminated on June 30, 1935, unless he qualified for promotion to assistant professor. She then examined other aspects of the case. Enrollment figures foreshadowed a further decline in the number of students in German courses; the department could no longer sustain a staff of five teachers. As the junior member in length of service, Bergel "was clearly indicated as the [one] to be discontinued." Still, the Dean consulted with Meder about Bergel's qualifications. They discussed evidence provided by the students' performance on the uniform examination, the failure of students to elect Bergel's advanced course, and complaints about his "uneven marking system." Meder told her that Bergel's personality "had not drawn either faculty or students to him and he had made no notable contribution to the life of the college outside the classroom." He had no scholarly publications.

The Dean then consulted the notes of her conversation with Hauptmann. He had told her that he tried to offer Bergel some suggestions on his teaching, but that his comments had been poorly received. Hauptmann also described his unfavorable observations when he had taken over Bergel's classes during the latter's illness. In view of these considerations, Corwin decided that she could not "conscientiously reverse the decision already reached by Acting-Dean Meder."[11]

Corwin took her findings to President Clothier. They agreed that the Dean should confirm the verbal dismissal in writing. Corwin did that in a letter to Bergel dated May 23, 1934. She wrote: "I learn . . . that Professor Hauptmann discussed your position with you last fall, after consultation with Dean Meder. This is merely to confirm the decision of the group that, in view of the lack of opportunity for your advancement here, you should plan to terminate your teaching at N.J.C. in June 1935."

Corwin invited Bergel to call on her for assistance in seeking another position. But her letter left a lot unsaid. She did not refer to Bergel's "deficiencies" or to any other factors that had influenced the decision.[12]

One of these factors was the status of Emil Jordan, the other instructor in the German Department. Jordan's appointment was also due to expire in 1935. But he had recently been recommended for promotion by Hauptmann, and his long-range prospects looked good. Less than two weeks after writing to Bergel, Dean Corwin assured Hauptmann that Jordan's name was "near the top of the list of those to be considered when we reach a more normal period of promotions and increases, both because of his worth as a teacher and his forthcoming publication."[13]

Whether they liked it or not, Bergel and Jordan were competing for the same academic slot. There was no chance that both would be promoted, and the administration's preference was decidedly for Jordan. Born in East Prussia in 1901, Jordan had received a doctorate in economics from the University of Koenigsberg and had taught at various "German colleges" in Brazil before immigrating to the United States in 1930. The following year he was appointed to an instructorship in German at N.J.C. Regarded as an able teacher, Jordan participated in the activities of the department and—equally important—he did not clash with the political views of Friedrich Hauptmann. He had just received the approval of the graduate faculty to offer a graduate course, and he was completing a textbook, *Kultur-Geographie von Deutschland,* which would get fine reviews upon its publication in 1935. Married to an N.J.C. alumnus, Jordan had applied for American citizenship several years before. Dean Corwin described him as a "very well adjusted, well balanced person." Put simply, his credentials allowed Hauptmann to make a plausible case that Jordan—and Jordan alone—merited promotion.[14]

Bergel did not acknowledge Corwin's letter. He was still recovering from his appendectomy and did not feel "strong enough to stand a very important discussion." When the two finally met—on September 26, 1934—Bergel asked why he was being dismissed. Corwin referred to the declining enrollments. Bergel was not satisfied. He wanted another meeting, with Hauptmann included, at which his "deficiencies" would be listed and explained.[15]

Corwin agreed to this, but Hauptmann did not, claiming that a confrontation would serve no useful purpose. Indeed, it would be "difficult for him to write letters of recommendation" for Bergel if they "should argue about the matter." In addition, Hauptmann did not have the time. He was about to leave for an extended stay in Germany.[16]

On October 1 Corwin received an angry letter from Sylvia Bergel. She said that before she had accepted her position at N.J.C. in 1931, she had been warned by the Institute of International Education that "the German Department was in the hands of a man without the education, experience, or cultural background usually required of a college teacher." Similar intimations had been given to her by a graduate professor at New York University "in whose department Professor Hauptmann had made tentative efforts to acquire the Ph.D degree." At N.J.C. she had found the students in her advanced courses so poorly prepared that she was obliged to reduce her standards below college level. She brought these matters to Corwin's attention, she said, because "Professor Hauptmann's aspersions against Mr. Bergel make it necessary."[17]

Corwin was not impressed. To her thinking, the letter was proof that Mrs. Bergel "and her husband had both accepted positions at N.J.C. without a feeling of loyalty to the College or the department which they were entering." Also, the letter seemed deceptive—even hypocritical—because Mrs. Bergel had recently sought a temporary job as Hauptmann's replacement while he was ill. Why would people who thought so little of the German Department want so badly to work there?[18]

Corwin met again—and alone—with Bergel in October. She told him that any discussion of his deficiencies was "academic"; it was necessary to reduce the size of the department, and the last person hired should be the first to go. Bergel left with the impression that if he continued to press the matter, he would receive no letters of recommendation for positions elsewhere. Corwin denied making any such statement, although she may have echoed Hauptmann's view that an unpleasant discussion would make it impossible to write positive letters.[19]

By this time, Bergel had been given several explanations for his dismissal. In September 1933 Hauptmann had told him that the department "wanted a change." A few weeks later, Albert Meder had informed him about the three-year rule and the preference for Jordan. In the fall of 1934 Dean Dorwin had emphasized declining enrollments and the need to reduce the teaching staff. At no point, however, did anyone discuss Bergel's "deficiencies" with Bergel himself. This is very important, because the young instructor believed that a teacher could be discharged only if he did his job poorly. And none of these explanations involved "incompetence."

The meetings with Corwin had a profound effect upon Bergel. "I felt from this moment on," he said later, "that I was no longer free to discuss the matter with officials of the University. . . . I was boiling inside." The decision to discharge him had been made in 1933 and reaffirmed in writing a year later. Yet Bergel was unwilling to accept it. He was determined to fight on. "Even a worm turns," he remarked sardonically, "even a bookworm turns."[20]

4 RUMORS

By October 1934 Lienhard Bergel at last understood that the college authorities had decided to dismiss him. But the more he brooded about his predicament, the more he became convinced that there could be only one explanation for it. He was the victim of political bias. Hauptmann was pro-Nazi; he was anti-Nazi. There had been no charges of incompetence; therefore, Hauptmann's action must have been political. From that point forward, two thoughts seemed to dominate Bergel's mind. One was the remote hope that he could remain at N.J.C. by replacing Mrs. Hauptmann.* The other was his determination to expose a shameful act of political discrimination.[1]

---

*One of the more interesting "economic" questions is whether the administration could have kept Jordan *and* Bergel on the faculty by firing Mrs. Hauptmann. Alan Silver, a critic of our 1985 Interim Report, insists that both men could have been retained by simply "dismissing" Mrs. Hauptmann and "postponing" Jordan's promotion. (See *Daily Targum*, January 21, 1987.) In reality, this scenario was impossible. As instructors, Jordan and Bergel were subject to the three-year rule. Unlike Mrs. Hauptmann, who held the rank of "assistant" at a very low salary, they could not be retained indefinitely in their present positions. They either had to be promoted or dismissed within a three-year period. (In exceptional cases, a fourth year could be granted by the Dean.) Silver has tried to get around this rule by arguing that it was not strictly enforced during the Depression. He is wrong. There is absolutely no evidence that any instructor at Rutgers University was kept on beyond four years without being promoted to the rank of assistant professor. In fact, the three-year rule (with a fourth-year option) was followed carefully. (See Dean Corwin, "Memorandum presented to Governor Hoffman," March 31, 1937; Clothier to Corwin, May 25, 1938; both in Clothier Papers, 143–223.) Silver is also wrong to assume that promotions to the rank of assistant professor were halted

That fall, Bergel began telling friends and colleagues about his predicament. The matter became a subject of conversation among the students. One of them, Zipporah Shapiro, recalled that some classmates had phoned her before the Christmas vacation to say that a mass meeting was being planned in Bergel's behalf. On the day she returned to school, Miss Shapiro met Bergel on the street and asked him whether he was being dropped for political reasons. He confirmed that this was the case. When students living in the German House related these stories to Miss Schlimbach, the directress, she called the seniors together. "I asked the girls to correct any misinformation they might hear," she later testified. "I told them that Mr. Bergel was being dismissed for economic reasons."[2]

Ironically, Hauptmann was not in New Brunswick at this time. In June 1934 he had requested a leave of absence for the coming semester. He had been ill, he said, and hoped to visit the spas in Germany to recover his health. In addition, he planned to secure a doctorate there. Hauptmann had begun working toward this goal at New York University, but because of the residency requirements it would take him two or three more years to secure the degree. He explained that in Germany he could complete the requirements in four or five months. This seemed rather implausible, even by the reduced standards of the new Nazi regime, but the Rutgers trustees approved his request to go abroad for "health and study." Hauptmann departed for Germany in October 1934.[3]

Why Hauptmann wanted a doctorate is not really clear. In the past, he had described the degree as irrelevant to his "qualifications for teaching." But now, with the presence of Bergel and Jordan, the junior men in the department had more impressive credentials than Hauptmann himself. It is possible, therefore, that he was driven by feelings of academic inferiority.

Hauptmann's stay in Germany was unusual, to say the least. He spent several weeks in Berlin, he wrote Miss Corwin, visiting

---

in this period. Between 1933 and 1937, eight instructors were promoted to assistant professor at N.J.C.; two were retained for a fourth year, as permitted under the three-year rule; and fifteen (including Bergel) were terminated at the end of the third year.

with "various government officials [who] wanted to have discussions with me." One of them was Ernst "Putzi" Hanfstaengl, the eccentric Harvard graduate who served as foreign press chief of the Nazi Party. Hanfstaengl was undoubtedly ignorant of Hauptmann's existence at this time. If the two men did have a discussion—and Hauptmann insisted in private and public that they did—then Hauptmann must have initiated it.[4]

Certainly, the motive was there. Hauptmann had arrived in Germany with a wildly impractical dissertation topic, "The Interrelations between German Art and Literature." He also had no contacts at Marburg, where he hoped to study, and a five-month deadline for completing his work. It is possible, therefore, that Hauptmann met with Hanfstaengl and other Nazi officials in order to ingratiate himself by revealing his political sympathies. Hauptmann understood that pressure exerted from Berlin might get him both a dissertation topic and a willing advisor at Marburg. Given the state of German universities in 1934—embroiled in mass purges of Jewish, Liberal, and Socialist professors—a simple communication from Hanfstaengl would be all that Hauptmann needed.[5]

At his "old beloved Marburg," Hauptmann worked under the supervision of Professor Max Deutschbein, a noted scholar of English literature. Hauptmann wrote Dean Corwin that Deutschbein had suggested a new dissertation topic for him: "A Scholarly Critique of German Instruction at the High Schools and Colleges of the United States." Even better, Hauptmann learned that all of his previous studies at German universities would be accepted in full. This meant that he could complete his remaining requirements within the time available to him.[6]

Hauptmann finished his dissertation in five months. It was a dreadful piece of work, even by Nazi standards of the day. He based his study on a handful of secondary sources. The research base was so thin that he attempted to pad it by "sending out questionnaires" to state Departments of Education in the United States. Hauptmann claimed that he received "comprehensive replies" and a "large number of syllabi" from these sources. Oddly, however, his final product made little use of these questionnaires, and there is real doubt as to whether he sent them at all. His dissertation may well have been a fraud.

This was not the worst of it. Sensing that scholarship was less important than ideological conformity, Hauptmann loaded his dissertation with pro-Nazi statements about Germany's "racial identity." At one point, for example, he claimed that fifteen million people of "German blood" in America, representing "some of the best elements of that population belonging to the German racial group," had been fighting for years to acquaint American schools "with the language and cultural values of their ancestral race." Hauptmann's sixty-nine-page dissertation contained 197 largely meaningless footnotes. Rather remarkably, no one at Rutgers—not even Lienhard Bergel—ever bothered to read this shoddy work.[7]

On the campus, meanwhile, there were occasional reminders of Adolf Hitler and his Third Reich. In September 1934 two Jewish refugees—Oscar Lassner from Leipzig and Leonid Kreutzer from Berlin—joined the music faculty at N.J.C. A few weeks later, Lienhard Bergel gave a well-received lecture on the relationship of Oswald Spengler's work to Nazi ideology. Of special significance, however, were the views expressed by Emily Hickman of the History Department. A popular, dynamic teacher, and an ardent member of the National Committee on the Cause and Cure of War, Hickman had toured Germany in the summer of 1934. She reported that the use of terror by the Nazis had been "very much misrepresented" in American newspapers. "The chief surprise to me," said Hickman, "was that something positive was going on in Germany." The people were united, working together, "and getting a great deal of happiness out of this knowledge." Hickman did not mention the persecution of Jews, the flight of intellectuals, or the military preparations. Her remarks did not provoke any rejoinders in the *Campus News*. From all indications, student sentiment toward the Nazis remained open-minded, with only small minorities in favor or in opposition.[8]

In January 1935 university officials got the first signs that the German Department was coming under attack. President Clothier received two anonymous letters complaining about pro-Nazi propaganda. He forwarded them to Dean Corwin, who discussed their contents with Emil Jordan, the acting department head in Hauptmann's absence. Jordan assumed that his own course, "German

Culture" was the likely target. He suggested that Corwin speak with "an intelligent young Jewish girl" in his class who would "be sensitive to any controversial material." Corwin decided to do nothing, however, "since Dr. Jordan had explained the matter satisfactorily." [9]

A few days later, President Clothier was visited by Harry S. Feller, a local businessman and a prominent figure in the New Brunswick Jewish community. Feller, who graduated with honors from Rutgers in 1908, had close ties to the University. He had heard about Bergel's predicament from his daughter, a student at N.J.C. He told Clothier that there was "disquiet among the Jewish residents in town on three scores": Bergel's dismissal; Emily Hickman's pro-Nazi remarks; and rumors that a graduate assistant had been denied employment at Rutgers because he was Jewish. Clothier promised to investigate the Bergel matter, and Feller agreed to seek more information about the graduate assistant. As for Miss Hickman, Clothier said there was nothing he could—or should—do. She had "entire freedom to say what she thinks and to express her opinion." [10]

The two anonymous letters had introduced the charge of pro-Nazi propaganda. Now the question of anti-Semitism had been raised. From this point forward, both issues were to figure prominently in the battle over Bergel's dismissal. For many in the Jewish community, Bergel was perceived as a "surrogate Jew" victimized for his opposition to the Nazis.

In the 1930s discrimination against Jews was very common in higher education and in the larger world beyond. Most colleges practiced "selective admissions," and some had well-defined quotas. This was especially true among the eastern schools, which feared that Jews would become the majority if religious barriers were eliminated. Authorities at Rutgers shared this apprehension. As a result, highly qualified Jewish students might be rejected while others with lesser qualifications would be admitted. [11]

These practices had been challenged in 1931 by a committee representing ten Jewish organizations in New Jersey. Chaired by Judge Joseph Siegler of Essex County, the committee prepared a brief that documented obvious instances of discrimination in admissions at the Men's Colleges. It showed that numerous Jewish applicants from high schools in Perth Amboy, Elizabeth, and New Brunswick had been rejected in 1930, while non-Jews with far inferior records had been accepted. The trustees did not dispute the committee's findings; they simply responded that the student body "should constitute a fairly representative cross section of the state . . . a composite and harmonious whole." That was the quota system, pure and simple. The proportion of Jewish students at the time was estimated to be between 12 and 15 percent.[12]

In the end, an acceptable compromise was negotiated. The University claimed that "there was no intention to discriminate against any class" and "no limitation . . . based on the percentage that such class might bear to the total population of the State." In short, the University said that it had not discriminated against Jews—but promised not to do it again. Judge Siegler accepted this assurance and announced that the controversy was over. His committee had made no charges against the Women's College, although there is evidence that discrimination prevailed there as well. In any case, the proportion of Jewish students at N.J.C. increased from 12.5 percent in 1930–1931 to 16.8 percent in 1934–1935. Ironically, Jews were overrepresented in German courses, where they made up more than one-third of the registrants until the academic year 1934–1935, when the proportion fell to about one-quarter.[13]

There also were problems at the faculty level. Jews constituted a handful of the Rutgers staff—mostly at the College of Agriculture—and rumors persisted that some deans would not hire them. There were virtually no Jewish professors at the men's colleges and only two—Lassner and Kreutzer—at N.J.C. These facts, so shocking today, were sadly common in the academic world of the 1930s. They reflected the attitudes and practices that restricted the access of Jews to the medical profession, to much of corporate business, to the most esteemed private clubs, and even to political preferment. Rutgers in the 1930s reflected the prevailing climate.[14]

Harry Feller did not want to embarrass his alma mater. He hoped to work quietly for change. After meeting with Clothier, he asked Bergel to prepare a statement that supported his charge of political discrimination. Bergel readily agreed; in late January he gave Feller a written report that he prepared with the assistance of his wife.[15]

It was a scathing indictment of Hauptmann. Bergel portrayed him as a volatile autocrat with poor academic training. Under his inept guidance, the department offered inferior instruction. Hauptmann was a bad teacher; his wife was worse. When Bergel took over Hauptmann's classes during the latter's illness, he found them "in an almost hopeless condition." Mrs. Hauptmann, meanwhile, gave "hopelessly difficult and unsuitable assignments." Department affairs were conducted irregularly; important decisions were usually made at Hauptmann's house. Miss Schlimbach was a testy woman who got whatever she wanted. Bergel himself was saddled with the heaviest teaching load, yet deprived of advanced courses.

More serious were the political charges. Hauptmann spent a lot of class time defending Hitler's policies and "correcting" misstatements about Germany in the American press. He had turned the students in the German House into Nazi supporters. He once told Bergel: "We Germans in America are living together in a small island in a hostile ocean. Contact with the enemy should be made only through . . . the captain of the group." Hauptmann was the captain, of course, and "disobedience was treachery." After Hitler came to power, Hauptmann remarked that he would not have hired Bergel had he known of his anti-Nazi views. He even suggested that Bergel return to Germany.

It was hardly surprising, then, that enrollments in German courses were declining. The political propaganda and the inept instruction were driving students away. "It is strange," Bergel concluded, "that I, the only non-Hitlerite of the German Department . . . am to lose my position because the Hitlerite propaganda of other members has caused a drop in registration."[16]

Feller delivered the statement to Clothier in March 1934. Attached to it was a second document that contained unflattering biographical sketches of the members of the N.J.C. German Department. Clothier passed on the material to Dean Corwin, who did not like—or believe—what she read. Corwin considered Bergel to be a bookish snob who judged everything by "the measuring rod of a German scholar." In her view, teaching a language to beginners did not require the exhaustive knowledge of philology that might be expected in classes for students preparing for the Ph.D. and state examinations in Germany. She added:

> We want our language faculty to impart something of the culture as well as the literature of the countries they represent. The more interests they have themselves, whether they be in music, in economics or in home life, the more they will have to share with their students. Above all, we want them to be real people. We consider mastery of subject matter only the starting point in our selection of teachers; in addition we count upon a generous contribution to the life at the college.

Measured by these standards, Corwin did not feel that the German Department offered inferior instruction. On the contrary, it was Bergel whom she found wanting.[17]

Bergel's statement only confirmed Corwin's impression that he was "rationalizing." "He was trying to find *outside himself* reasons for his non-reappointment." He was reading motives into other people's actions where I could not find them." Obviously, Corwin did not believe that Bergel had been fired for political reasons, or that Hauptmann's classes were filled with Nazi propaganda. Within a few days, she returned the documents to President Clothier with her conclusions.

Clothier wrote promptly to Feller. He reported Corwin's findings, explained the three-year rule, and added that "a careful appraisal of [Bergel's work] has confirmed the judgment that he has not qualified for promotion." Clothier then dismissed the charges of religious and political discrimination by noting that N.J.C. had just appointed two Jewish refugees to the Music Department. The University, he said, "had an openminded attitude toward all points of view."[18]

Clothier had now been drawn into the most serious controversy of his early presidential years. A member of a prominent Philadelphia family, a Princeton graduate, and a lieutenant colonel during World War I, he had entered the educational field in 1923 as assistant headmaster of Haverford School. From there, Clothier had moved to the University of Pittsburgh in 1929 to become Dean of Men. Strongly recommended for the Rutgers post by the presidents of Pittsburgh, Princeton, Pennsylvania, and Northwestern, he assumed his new responsibilities in March 1932.

Clothier's beliefs and manners were decidedly patrician. He was cordial, gracious, and remarkably good-looking. As an educator, he believed that universities should develop the "social-cultural-spiritual qualities" of students, not simply their intellects. As an administrator, he preferred order to innovation, although he encouraged original scholarship on the part of his most creative faculty members. He was, by nature, cautious and attentive to detail. His numerous speeches—even his letters—were well crafted, frequently revised, and carefully expressed. His greatest strength was the force of his personality, and on it his leadership was based.[19]

Clothier's letter to Feller, like Meder's earlier letter to Professor Braun, had an unfortunate history. After submitting his statement, Bergel phoned Feller frequently to learn the President's response. Finally, Feller called him to his office and said that the letter had arrived. Bergel found Feller in much distress—"quite broken down"—and unwilling to divulge the contents because he did not want to hurt Bergel's feelings. Very soon thereafter, Bergel spoke with Professor Selman A. Waksman, who had been in communication with Feller.* According to Bergel, Waksman informed him that an "investigation" had shown him to be an "incompetent teacher." Bergel was shocked by the charge of "incompetence"— which, of course, was not in Clothier's letter—and by the fact that the "investigation" had provided him with no opportunity to respond. Harry Feller's kindly intervention had left him more outraged and desperate than before.[20]

At this very moment, events beyond the Rutgers campus were shaping the manner in which the Bergel case would be pursued.

---

*Professor Waksman was an eminent microbiologist at the College of Agriculture. He would win the Nobel Prize in 1952 for his discovery of streptomycin, the conqueror of tuberculosis. Waksman was one of Bergel's strongest defenders. An outspoken opponent of Nazism, he had denounced the Hitler regime in speeches on

The revelations of the McCormack-Dickstein Committee about pro-Hitler activities in America were now front-page news. So, too, were the demonstrations of local Nazi groups, which often ended violently. In Irvington, an angry crowd attacked a meeting of FONG with clubs, stones, and stench bombs. Police units from Newark were forced to quell the fighting. In Hoboken, three thousand members of German-American organizations, some wearing swastika armbands, held an enthusiastic parade. They were greeted by the mayor and other dignitaries, who acknowledged the Nazi salute as each unit passed by. The festivities ended with the singing of the Star Spangled Banner and the Nazi Anthem, the Horst Wessell song.[21]

As public apprehension mounted, the New Jersey Legislature passed—and the governor signed—the so-called Anti-Nazi Law of 1935. The measure made it a misdemeanor to disseminate statements which promoted "hatred, violence, or hostility against any group . . . by reason of race, color, religion or manner of worship." A few days later, the lawmakers prescribed a loyalty oath for public-school teachers and college faculties supported by public funds. The main targets, of course, were the pro-Hitler—and anti-Semitic—groups in the state.[22]

It was against this background that Lienhard and Sylvia Bergel decided to seek the assistance of influential legislators and other prominent officials. On the day the Anti-Nazi Law received the governor's signature, Mrs. Bergel sent a personal note to State Senator C. E. Loiseaux. In it, she described Hauptmann as an "ardent Nazi" who "strongly advocated Hitlerism, in the classroom as well as elsewhere," and claimed that Bergel was being dismissed and labeled as incompetent because of his political views. Referring to the new law, she said it was unjust that her husband should be forced out "under a cloud because he is the only anti-Nazi in the German Department." Loiseaux, who chaired the Appropriations Committee, was one of several legislators to receive this message.[23]

At Rutgers, meanwhile, student activists were gaining in

---

the Rutgers campus. Waksman met frequently with Bergel during the crisis, to offer his counsel and support.

strength. Appalling economic conditions, the failure of disarmament efforts, the fear of fascism abroad—all contributed to stir the campuses from their customary political lethargy. In October 1934 students in New Brunswick formed a New Jersey Division of the American Youth Congress. Despite some internal dissension, the delegates passed resolutions demanding the abolition of R.O.T.C., the withdrawal of American troops from all "colonial countries," the adoption of unemployment insurance, and a boycott of the Berlin Olympics in 1936.[24]

In November a chapter of the left-wing National Student League was organized on campus. Its leader, Alan Silver, announced that the NSL intended to fight "fascist tendencies, race discrimination, suppression of student thought, and anti-peace activity." There was a need, he declared, for a national student organization that was "definitely radical in its point of view." The nation's economy was in chaos and he foresaw "the approach of fascism on the American horizon."[25]

Bergel's cause had an obvious appeal for the NSL. It involved the explosive Nazi issue; it had a local dimension; and it came at a perfect time, only weeks before the national student "peace strike" of 1935. At Rutgers, this protest against "war and fascism" was sponsored by a number of groups, but dominated by the NSL. *Campus News*, the N.J.C. student paper, said: "It is a strike promoted by the National Student League, a communist organization, which has hitherto exhibited little interest in peace, but is notoriously opposed to fascism."[26]

Bergel had learned from several students that the NSL was planning to protest his dismissal. They also told him that the group was loaded with "radicals and communists." Bergel was disturbed by the news; he went to the house on Handy Street where the strike planners were assembled. There he met Alan Silver, who said: "We want to do something for you; we want to hold a mass demonstration." Bergel begged them to call it off. "I told them, first, that the idea of a mass meeting did not appeal to me at all," he testified, "and, second, that I did not want to appear connected with any special organization, whatever character it was."[27]

Bergel's student supporters at N.J.C. were also opposed to a mass meeting. They did not want "radical" Rutgers men intervening in a matter that concerned the College for Women, and they did not wish to injure their cause by becoming involved with left-wing elements on the campus. When efforts were made by Silver and his allies to stage a demonstration for Bergel at N.J.C., they were quickly rebuffed.[28]

On April 12, 1935, the well-planned "peace strike" was held on the campus of the New Brunswick Theological Seminary. It was an orderly affair, attended by more than 350 students. There was no demonstration for Bergel. On April 13 *Campus News* printed a brief item about the return of Professor Hauptmann from his leave of absence in Germany. The same issue contained a letter that raised questions about Bergel's dismissal, along with an editorial that attempted to supply the answers.[29]

The letter, sent anonymously by an "interested group," called upon the administration to clear up "false rumors and misunderstandings" about Bergel's dismissal. They were:

(1) That a reduction in the student enrollment necessitates a cut in that department.
(2) That the professor is inefficient.
(3) That the political differences within the department are responsible for this dismissal.

The first rumor, the letter went on, "is certainly refuted in our daily classroom where we are being taught that the spread of employment is preferable to reduction in personnel." (In a thinly veiled reference to Mrs. Hauptmann, the writers argued that "preference should be given to the sole supporter of a family, regardless of seniority.") The second rumor was "disproved by [Bergel's] reputation among his students . . . as a thorough and considerate instructor who has shown himself valuable in both the classroom and in campus activities." The third rumor was not even worthy of consideration, "since we know that a liberal college would not countenance any political interference." Why, then, had Bergel been terminated? A "reasonable explanation" was owed to the student body.[30]

The *Campus News* editorial—"Rebuttal and Redress"—tried

to provide that explanation. After drafting it, the editor met with Dean Corwin, who "gave her a broad view of the situation, so that she might be able to form a more accurate impression." The editor explained, somewhat incorrectly, that all members of the faculty were subject to annual reappointment, and that Bergel had been informed about two years previously "that he could expect no promotion here." Because enrollments in German were declining, the staff had to be reduced. Bergel, as the junior in point of service, would not be "invited" to teach another year. Regarding the political issue, "the Administration [had] affirmed that to the best of its knowledge, it believes that this phase of the question is not influencing the decision." The editor was impressed by Corwin's "sincere explanation." She also complimented Bergel on the "high quality of his work as professor" and wished him well in the future.[31]

This editorial was extremely important. Rather than stifling the controversy, it served to introduce it to the campus as a whole. The case was now out in the open. It had entered a new phase.

Nearly two years had passed since Bergel was informed, verbally, that he would not be promoted. The initial decision had been made within the context of the University's dire financial and enrollment problems, the three-year rule, and the preference for Emil Jordan as the instructor to be retained. The extent to which Hauptmann's personal and political differences with Bergel were involved is, of course, as critical as it is problematical. When Dean Corwin confirmed this decision in May 1934, the same factors were in place. Economic conditions within the University had worsened, and the Dean felt that a cut in the German Department would have to be made. These factors, in her analysis, overshadowed Bergel's alleged deficiencies as a faculty member at N.J.C.

Bergel always believed that his appointment could be terminated only on the basis of "incompetence," and he made repeated efforts to learn what "charges" there were against him. In fact, there were no charges; he was never accused of incompetence. Although he later claimed to have told Meder and Corwin of his suspicion that political discrimination was involved in his dismissal, there is no evidence to support this statement.[32]

After his conference with Dean Corwin in October 1934, Bergel's case rapidly took on larger dimensions. He now told his friends and colleagues that he was the victim of political discrimination. He and Mrs. Bergel tried to enlist the interest of important people outside the University. Radical students sought to take up the cause. The touchy issues of Nazi propagandizing and anti-Semitism were brought into the controversy. Questions were raised about Mrs. Hauptmann's employment. On the other side, key administrators shared Dean Corwin's irritation at Bergel's determined refusal to accept his dismissal quietly. Thus the affair stood in mid-April 1935.

Old Queens

College Hall on NJC campus

Friedrich J. Hauptmann

Lienhard Bergel

President Robert C. Clothier

J. Edward Ashmead

Acting Dean Albert Meder

Dean Margaret T. Corwin

5 THE CRISIS

In retrospect, it is easy to understand why the Bergel case generated so much sympathy in 1935. The findings of the McCormack-Dickstein Committee, and the ugly activities of some German-American groups, had sensitized the public to the dangers of Hitlerism at home. New Jersey had responded by passing an "anti-Nazi Law." On the N.J.C. campus, a young opponent of fascism had been discharged under questionable circumstances. He was facing unemployment in the midst of a terrible depression. And the Rutgers administration had put forth no convincing explanation for his dismissal.

For the moment, public debate was limited to the *Campus News*. On April 24 a second letter appeared, written by "another interested group." The letter called Bergel a teacher of "superlative excellence" and urged that he be given Mrs. Hauptmann's job. The following week, "A Group of German Students" claimed that Bergel, "the best teacher and a scholar in the department," had been fired by Hauptmann, "a vigorous Nazi supporter," for political reasons. The letter added: "Most of our instructors are Nazi sympathizers [who] expend quite some time and energy in injecting Nazi propaganda into their classes. . . . Is it any wonder if many students prefer not to take German under these circumstances?"[1]

The airing of these matters obviously displeased the College administration. Albert Meder, who now served as faculty advisor to *Campus News*, discussed his concerns with Dean Corwin. She agreed that he should "point out to the editor that no good would come of these repeated letters." Meder spoke with the editor, Marion Short, and found that "she was concerned about the possible

suppression of free speech if she refrained from printing [them]."
When Meder offered to assist her in reviewing these letters, Miss
Short firmly declined.[2]

Meder had more success with Friedrich Hauptmann, who was
calling him almost daily for advice. Meder told Hauptmann to "say
and do absolutely nothing," and the professor agreed. The problem, however, was that Hauptmann's student supporters, many of
whom lived in the German House, were eager to make *their* views
known. When Hauptmann learned that they were seeking signa-
tures to a letter in his behalf, he sent them to Meder. Their letter
was, in Meder's words, "a masterpiece of invective" that belonged
in the wastebasket. He suggested that they shorten the document
and "state facts." The students redrafted the letter, showed the re-
visions to Meder, accepted his suggestions, and then circulated it
among the German classes, except those taught by Bergel.[3]

The letter, which appeared in *Campus News* on May 8, was
relatively mild. The writers did not concern themselves with Bergel's dismissal. Their objective was to defend Hauptmann and the
German Department against "statements based on prejudices, as-
sumptions, [and] rumors." They denied that there had been any
Nazi propagandizing in the German classes, and they challenged
anyone to cite a case where a student had been discriminated
against because of political differences with a teacher. When questions were raised about Nazism, they said, instructors responded
only with statements of fact; discussion was never stifled. In clos-
ing, the writers made a plea "for the type of freedom of expression
which is based on truth, good judgment and good taste."[4]

The letter, sent by "seventy" unnamed German students, was
followed by a stronger one from a group of nine alumnae. Appear-
ing in *Campus News*, it lashed out at Bergel as well as his student
supporters. Bergel was not the best teacher in the department, the
alumnae declared. For one thing, he had shown "a great deal of
favoritism in his classes"; for another, he—and he alone—had expressed political opinions in his lectures. Shocked at finding such
"bold untruths" in the college paper, the alumnae expressed the
hope that it would not happen again.[5]

In response, Bergel's supporters circulated a petition of their own. Calling him "one of the best members of the German Department and thoroughly competent to teach German at N.J.C.," it was signed by 405 of the 892 students enrolled at the College. More than half of these students had never taken a German course; only 87 had actually been in Bergel's classes. Quite obviously, then, the instructor's cause had generated widespread sympathy for both his personal plight and his political position.[6]

Although *Campus News* did not publish the names of the signers, a list did accompany the petition. In particular, the college administration was interested in knowing how many of these students were Jewish, how many had taken political science courses, and how many were students of Hauptmann. An analysis of the names showed that 99 of the 150 Jewish students at the College (or 66 percent) had signed the petition, while only 41 percent of the non-Jewish students had signed. A large number of the students had taken political science courses (76), and a small number had taken courses with Hauptmann (29). These figures were significant to N.J.C. officials, because a number of them believed that Jewish students and "radical" political science instructors were behind the Bergel controversy.[7]

These letters and petitions were fueled by new developments in the case. Soon after his return from Germany, Professor Hauptmann had "inadvertently" left a stack of pamphlets on a desk in the German Department. He had obtained them, he later testified, from someone at the men's college and had not yet read them. The pamphlets—*A Foreign Visitor's Impressions of Germany*—were written by Clarence G. Campbell, president of the so-called Eugenics Research Association. Campbell, an avowed racist, had strong ties to the Nazi government in Berlin. He corresponded frequently with Nazi officials, who praised his work and even invited him to attend the huge Nuremberg Rally in November 1936. In his pamphlet, Campbell endorsed key Nazi policies, including the efforts to secure and protect the Aryan racial purity of the German people. This was hardly surprising; Campbell had been working for several years to launch a "Pan Aryan League," where member-nations would cooperate with one another in dealing with the "Jewish danger."[8]

Students picked up copies of the pamphlet, as did some professors with offices in the building. Within days, the campus was buzzing about Hauptmann's latest pro-Nazi "propaganda blitz." Dean Corwin learned about it from a curious newspaper reporter. She called Hauptmann, who explained that he had accidentally left the pamphlets on the table while using the telephone. He sent a copy to Corwin and removed the rest. But serious damage had been done to his credibility.[9]

As the campus debate continued, Bergel sought the aid of other state officials. In mid-April he wrote to State Senator John E. Toolan, who invited him to his Perth Amboy office. Toolan, impressed with Bergel's sincerity, sent a letter to President Clothier. Although he did not believe that Rutgers would dismiss an instructor for political reasons, Toolan remarked that, if Bergel's charges were true, "then the chief of the department, not the subordinate, should be dismissed." In his reply, Clothier explained the three-year rule and said: "The fact that Mr. Bergel has not been reappointed should not be regarded as a sign of incompetence to teach. It is, however, a sign that he has not demonstrated his fitness for promotion to the rank of assistant professor and is not desired as a continuing member of the staff."[10]

Toolan did not pursue the matter, but Bergel did. He wrote letters to Charles Elliot, the Commissioner of Education, and to Horace Prall, the president of the State Senate. Both men were *ex-officio* trustees of the University. In his letters, Bergel repeated the familiar charges and added some new ones as well. He criticized Hauptmann for keeping his wife on the staff and for obtaining a suspicious Ph.D. at Marburg in only four months. He noted that Hauptmann was not a citizen, while he—Bergel—had an American wife and son and would acquire citizenship in two years. He also sent along copies of the Campbell pamphlets as "tangible proof that Mr. Hauptmann was interested in winning students to the Nazi point of view."[11]

Bergel's student advocates were also active in approaching public officials. On May 1 a delegation met in New Brunswick with Assemblyman John J. Rafferty, a sponsor of the "Anti-Nazi Law." They gave him "a long statement as to pro-Nazi activities at the College." He told them to see President Clothier; if they did not secure redress, they could file an ordinary criminal complaint. When Clothier learned of this meeting, he sent Rafferty a letter almost identical to the one he had written to Senator Toolan.[12]

Outside agencies were drawn into the matter. Late in April Dean Corwin received a letter from an official of Consumers' Research. Was it true, the official asked, that Bergel had been dropped because of his political beliefs? Corwin sent the letter to Clothier, who replied that Bergel had not "demonstrated the necessary qualities as a teacher." The decision to dismiss him, therefore, had "nothing whatever to do with any political belief . . . he may or may not hold." Clothier's letter was made available to Bergel, who saw it as reviving the "charge of incompetence" against him.[13]

These were difficult times for Hauptmann as well. When he went abroad in October, the campus had been calm; now it was seething with activity, much of it directed against him. He tried to follow Meder's counsel to "say and do absolutely nothing." When he came under attack in the *Campus News*, President Clothier called him in to discuss the accusations that Bergel had made. Hauptmann denied them all, including the charge that he once told Bergel he would not have hired him had he known of his opposition to Hitler. Apparently, Clothier was satisfied with the answers.[14]

Hauptmann also had a disturbing encounter with Professor Harold Van Dorn, a political scientist at N.J.C. The two men had been friends, despite wide political disagreements between them. Van Dorn was known as a liberal activist; a talk he gave at a chapel program, which called for a redistribution of wealth in the United States, had aroused considerable comment. He was an ardent supporter of Bergel, whom he viewed as a victim of Hauptmann's pro-Nazi politics. According to Hauptmann, Van Dorn had warned him that the state legislature was now alarmed about Nazi activities. He implied that Bergel's termination could have detrimental consequences. Hauptmann, regarding Van Dorn's remarks as a threat, reported the conversation to university officials.[15]

On May 3 the campus controversy reached the public press for the first time. It came in the form of a letter to the *Daily Home*

News by an "interested party"—most likely the parent of a student at N.J.C. The writer had heard about "strange goings-on in the German Department." There was "talk of Fascistic propaganda, of dismissal of a competent and well-liked German professor because of political, or . . . more definitely, Nazi discrimination, etc." A few days later, the newspaper printed a letter by a recent graduate that described Bergel as the most valuable teacher in the department. It would be a terrible injustice, the writer added, if Bergel were discharged on grounds of incompetence.[16]

Despite these many efforts, the Rutgers authorities were not inclined to alter their decision—or even to explain carefully how they had made it. The academic year was drawing to a close. Time was running out for Bergel. What more could be done?

The answer was supplied by Alan Silver. Over the next two weeks, he would play the leading role in bringing the Bergel case to national attention. A local resident and a member of the senior class at the Men's College, "Buddy"—as he was known—came from "a good, bourgeois Jewish family." During his freshman year at Rutgers, alarmed by the state of the world, he had become involved in left-wing causes. His experiences had taught him that most campus radicals were talkers, not doers. Since the young Communists were exempt from this failing, Silver cast his lot with the National Student League. He was a natural leader who believed in getting things done. When the efforts of the NSL seemed to be getting nowhere, he decided to act on his own.[17]

On May 4, a Friday, he called on Fraser Metzger, the Dean of Men, with whom he had had many previous encounters. He told Metzger that a group of N.J.C. students were demanding a public investigation. Unless the University agreed to this demand by Monday, the students would take their plea to the legislature, with potentially damaging consequences for the Rutgers appropriation. If the University did agree to a public probe, Silver thought he could persuade the women not to go to Trenton. His account of the threatened action, he later acknowledged, was a "right-out lie," which he made up as the conversation went along. But it had the desired effect.[18]

On Monday morning Silver received word that President Clothier wanted to see him. Though the details of their conversation are not known, Clothier did express his willingness to meet with Bergel. Silver promptly relayed the message, and Bergel made an appointment for that afternoon.[19]

Bergel's discussion with Clothier, by his own account, was a lengthy one. Bergel wanted to know the reasons for his dismissal; the President replied that Rutgers was under no obligation to provide them. Bergel did not accept this view; he wanted a proper investigation made of his competence.

The issue of Nazi propaganda came up. Bergel recalled that "President Clothier said Professor Hauptmann has a right to make as much propaganda as he likes on this campus." (It seems more likely that Clothier said that Hauptmann, like anyone else, was entitled to express his political views.) On the matter most directly at issue, Clothier supposedly told Bergel: "I shall not reopen your case; however, I shall review it. I tell you I will not change the decision arrived at, but if you have anything additional to add to your report [to Feller], then you hand it in and I shall be glad to see it."[20]

In the next few days, President Clothier consulted with administrators and faculty members about the case. He was fully aware of student pressures, the interest of local citizens, the approaches to influential legislators, and the threat that had been fabricated by Alan Silver. The president was especially apprehensive at this time because the annual appropriation was still awaiting final action. He hoped to avoid an explosion that could severely damage the University.[21]

By Saturday, May 11, Clothier had decided to appoint a special committee of trustees to conduct a hearing. There were precedents for this procedure. The year before, an associate professor of geology had attempted to rescind his resignation, claiming it was made under duress. A trustee committee had met for three hours, heard the professor, and then voted him down. Bergel learned of the president's decision from Selman Waksman. He was obviously pleased. At last—after two years of trying—he would be told the reasons for his dismissal.[22]

But Alan Silver was not finished. In fact, he was just warming up. After meeting with Dean Metzger, he phoned Mrs. Bergel to ask whether he could contact the American Civil Liberties Union in Bergel's behalf. She said that would be fine; she had thought about doing it herself. So Silver went ahead and brought the ACLU into the case.[23]

On May 10 Bergel met with the ACLU's Committee on Academic Freedom in New York City. The committee—which included such prominent figures as Roger Baldwin, Reinhold Niebuhr, and Sidney Hook—had a lengthy agenda that day. After interrogating Bergel for ten or fifteen minutes, it decided to inform President Clothier that the case was under investigation and to send a delegation to meet with him in New Brunswick.[24]

On May 12 Clothier received a startling letter from the ACLU. It claimed that the Committee on Academic Freedom had obtained a "full-report" from an investigator about the Bergel case. The report revealed that Bergel had been given conflicting reasons for his dismissal—"economy" and "incompetence," among them—and that the German Department was "under the domination of persons with Nazi sympathies." References were made to Hauptmann's sojourn in Marburg, the circulation of Campbell's notorious pamphlet, and reports that Hauptmann preached "the glories of Nazi Germany" in his classes. The committee also claimed that Clothier had expressed his "chagrin that . . . [Bergel] had not been able to change his views and accept the Nazi philosophy and policies." On the basis of these findings, the committee had voted to support Bergel's plea for reinstatement and to pursue the charge that the German Department had engaged in Nazi propaganda.

The final paragraph was blunt and threatening:

Before we take any final action . . . we believe it important to secure your statement of the situation. We have therefore requested our New Jersey representative to confer with you over the weekend. We trust that you will see him . . . for if the charges made above are left unanswered by the college administration we believe it appropriate to protest to the legislature against the appropriation of any money to a state educational institution in which a department so openly disseminates foreign propaganda, suppresses free speech and discriminates against students and staff members for their views.[25]

Clothier was appalled by the charges—and threats—contained in this letter. He fired back a telegram, saying he had just appointed a committee to hear Bergel's charges, and he would never permit the dismissal of a teacher because of his political views. "Shall be glad to cooperate," he concluded, "and request cooperation in return."[26]

On May 13 Clothier had dinner with three ACLU representatives at his New Brunswick home. According to one account—prepared by Abraham Isserman, the ACLU attorney—the group agreed on certain conclusions. They were: that Hauptmann was pro-Nazi; that Bergel was anti-Nazi; that the political differences between them preceded Bergel's first termination notice; and that Bergel claimed his dismissal was politically motivated.

Clothier argued that the drop in German enrollments had forced the College to release one member of the staff. The choice had fallen on Bergel because he was the junior member and because he lacked "certain characteristics" required in good teaching. But Clothier "admitted that perhaps Professor Hauptmann's antipathy to Bergel was the cause of the recommendation that he be dismissed," Isserman wrote. "He stated that he too desired to sift the controversy to the bottom."

The discussion then shifted to the format of the hearing. The ACLU representatives suggested that interested students and faculty members be invited to testify. Clothier readily agreed. He also proposed that the ACLU send an observer to hear the testimony and question the witnesses. The ACLU readily agreed. These two additions were to give the hearing a very different character from those conducted by previous trustee committees.[27]

The day after this meeting, another bombshell exploded. Alan Silver was a reader of the *New York World Telegram*. He especially admired one of the paper's reporters, Frederick E. Woltman, whose journalistic talents were to earn him three Pulitzer prizes. In a well-publicized incident, Woltman had been fired as a graduate assistant at the University of Pittsburgh in 1929 for "radical activities." He was promptly hired by the *World Telegram*. Silver decided that Woltman would be interested in the Bergel case. He sent him some material about the controversy, and Woltman followed up the lead. On May 15 he interviewed Bergel and Clothier by telephone. That afternoon his story was published under the headline, "Rutgers Fires German Prof. as Anti-Nazi."[28]

Woltman highlighted the conflict between the pro-Nazis in the German Department and the anti-Nazi instructor. Bergel was quoted extensively about his grievances and his charge that Hitlerite propaganda had been circulated on the N.J.C. campus. As an example, he cited the Campbell pamphlet. Woltman referred to the upcoming hearing, the new "Anti-Nazi Law," and the pending state appropriation for Rutgers. His story had a tremendous impact.[29]

Bergel claimed that he "almost fell on the floor when [he] saw what was in the paper." That afternoon he was besieged by reporters who were eager to get in on Woltman's scoop. He had a surprising visitor as well, Stephen Birmingham, who identified himself as an investigator for the McCormack-Dickstein Committee. Birmingham was interested in Nazi propaganda, and Bergel gave him a copy of the infamous Campbell pamphlet. For the next few months, during the trustee hearing and after, Birmingham would play a mysterious role in Bergel's affairs.[30]

To this point, Clothier had not defined the scope or object of the inquiry. He first believed the committee should "determine if good and valid reasons exist for Mr. Bergel's non-reappointment." He revised this to read: "determine if reasons exist why Mr. Bergel should not be reappointed," which was significantly different. But then Clothier returned to his original position. His final charge to the committee members asked them to "determine if the reasons for the failure of the administration to reappoint Dr. Lienhard Bergel for 1935–36 are good and valid."[31]

Of course, Clothier understood that more was involved here than the decision to dismiss a single instructor. As he told the chairman of the trustee committee, "I suspect we shall have to have *two hearings:*

(a) To determine if "good and valid" cause exists for not reappointing Bergel.

(b) To determine if the German Department is violating the Pesin [Anti-Nazi] Law or other anti-propaganda legislation.

Given the press reports about Hauptmann, the Campbell pamphlet, and the pro-Nazi activities at N.J.C., point "b" would have to be confronted.[32]

The first official notice that Bergel received about the hearing came in a letter of May 11 from Clothier. The letter referred to their meeting several days before and asked whether Bergel intended to submit a statement to the special committee of trustees. No mention was made of the scope or format of the hearing, or when it would be held. Bergel reminded Clothier that he had already submitted a statement through Harry Feller. "Moreover," he wrote, "at the interview on Monday you specifically stated that you would not reopen the matter and that even if you did review it, you would not change the verdict already arrived at."[33]

Bergel went on to say that he would be glad to prepare another statement, but that he wanted to offer oral evidence as well. "Naturally," he added, "I wish to learn what the charges against me are, and to have the opportunity to defend myself against them." Clothier responded, testily, by reminding Bergel that "no charges have been brought against you." However, he also agreed to the instructor's crucial request that he be represented by counsel at the hearing. A lawyer was needed, said Bergel, because he had considerable material to present and many witnesses to be questioned.[34]

Clothier had strong feelings about the case. Having repeatedly stated that Bergel did not possess the proper attributes for a member of the Rutgers faculty, he now felt obliged to codify his thinking on this matter. There were four criteria, he concluded, by which teachers should be judged: academic competence, general usefulness, loyalty to the institution, and personality.[35]

Faculty members, said Clothier, should be well-trained professionals who demonstrate excellence as teachers and potential growth as scholars. They should put welfare of the University ahead of personal advantage. They should work in friendly cooperation with their colleagues, "capable of differing with them in opinion and viewpoint . . . without impugning the integrity and sincerity of their motives." Faculty members should feel a responsibility to contribute to the social and cultural life of the campus, to show initiative in college activities, and to share in necessary routine work. Finally, they should have the personal qualities appropriate to these goals, such as "integrity, attractiveness of appearance and manner, graciousness, tact and a sense of humor, to mention just a few."[36]

In baccalaureate addresses at both N.J.C. and the men's colleges that June Clothier also expressed his thoughts on the general issue of freedom of speech. Noting that those who had settled early in New England to achieve religious freedom soon set about persecuting persons of differing beliefs, he observed that the same tendencies were now evident. "The truth is that when you suppress discussion which espouses a certain point of view you do not alter the sentiment back of that discussion," he told the seniors at N.J.C. "You generate pressure which is only too likely to break out elsewhere in far more violent forms." In his remarks to the men, Clothier dealt with the question of propaganda, which he defined as "anything . . . anyone may say which you don't believe." Propaganda and free speech were in eternal conflict. "Where these controversies exist no court of arbitration can be as effective as a spirit of mutual tolerance, well oiled by a sense of humor." In an obvious reference to the local imbroglio, he added:

> Charges that the principle of freedom of speech is being violated crop up here and there all over the country. Usually these charges have their origin in the thought that someone suspects that someone else differs with him in endeavoring to keep him from saying what he believes. Right there is evidence that he has taken leave of his sense of humor; so he protests and then his opponent in the controversy protests in return—and these two utterly sincere and usually intelligent persons create a Roman holiday for all who have retained their sense of humor to witness and enjoy.[37]

Despite these words, however, the president's mood was grim. The press accounts of the case had inspired a stream of mail to his office. Resolutions supporting Bergel arrived from groups as diverse as the Retail Merchants Division of the local Chamber of Commerce and the Brooklyn College Chapter of the National Student League. There also were letters from Jews, anti-Semites, concerned parents, students, alumnae and faculty members of the University. These letters, often passionate in tone, ran largely in Bergel's favor.[38]

As the hearings approached, it appeared that Bergel had attained his objectives. He had long clamored to be told the reasons for his termination and to have the opportunity to answer any charges that might be brought against him. In fact, however, there were no charges brought against him. Although the ostensible purpose of the hearing was to determine whether "good and valid reasons" existed for his non-reappointment, the committee quickly redefined its mission. It would now investigate Bergel's charges of political discrimination and Nazi propagandizing—thereby turning Friedrich Hauptmann into the defendant. That the initial decision in June 1933 had involved an evaluation of the relative merits of Lienhard Bergel and Emil Jordan as candidates for eventual promotion, with the choice falling on the latter, was almost totally ignored. An academic incident had assumed political dimensions. In a broader sense, Rutgers University was to be on trial, accused of being soft on Nazism and hostile to those who opposed Hitler's doctrines.

6 THE HEARINGS

The five members of the Special Trustees Committee, chosen
by President Clothier, could hardly have imagined what lay
before them on the afternoon of May 21, 1935. They had come to
the Rutgers administration building, Old Queens, expecting to decide a simple matter in a short period of time. Two months and
twenty-one sessions later, they had listened to 110 witnesses de-
liver more than a million words of testimony.

The Trustees Committee consisted of Chairman J. Edward
Ashmead, Philip M. Brett, Miriam Lippincott, John Wycoff Mettler, and Dr. John Raven of the New Brunswick Theological Seminary. The dominant figures—Brett, Mettler, and Ashmead—were
among the most powerful and devoted alumni of the University; all
were attorneys. Brett, a football hero and former acting president of
Rutgers, was a descendant of Philip Milledoler, who had presided
over the College a century before. Mettler, a trustee since 1916,
headed the Interwoven Stocking Company of New Brunswick, the
largest manufacturer of men's hosiery in the world. Ashmead, a
graduate of Harvard Law School and a partner in the Newark firm
of Lindabury, Depue, and Faulks, was a life trustee of Rutgers and
vice-president of the Alumni Association. "He told me once that he
owed a great debt to the college," another trustee said of Ashmead.
"He has taken his place among our great alumni: great in sense of
loyalty, and service, and inspiring leadership."[1]

The hearings were regularly attended by Dr. Albert Meredith
of the state Board of Regents; Assemblyman Samuel Pesin of Hud-
son County; Stephen Birmingham of the McCormack-Dickstein
Committee staff; and observers from the American Civil Liberties

Union, the American Legion, and the Steuben Society. President Clothier, Dean Corwin, and Albert Meder came to many sessions, as did members of the N.J.C. faculty and the press corps. Bergel and Hauptmann, the two principals of the hearings, were both represented by counsel. Professor Bergel's attorney, Sidney J. Kaplan, worked for Morgan and Lockwood, a New York law firm known for its liberal sympathies. Kaplan had been involved in a number of civil rights cases, including the famous Scottsboro trials of the early 1930s. His services were provided free of charge by the ACLU.[2]

Hauptmann was represented by Fred G. Tauber of Jersey City. Tauber, a customs attorney, had run unsuccessfully for Congress as a Republican in 1934. How and why Hauptmann chose him is not known. There may have been an ethnic connection because Tauber had represented German companies and German nationals in the United States. What *is* known, however, is that Tauber charged the professor about $1,500 for his services.[3]

The ground rules for the hearings had been carefully defined by the principals and their attorneys. Both sides had the right to call witnesses. Interested students, alumni, and faculty members were encouraged to testify under oath about their knowledge of the controversy. Witnesses were allowed to read an opening statement to the committee. They would then be questioned by Chairman Ashmead and the other trustees. Dr. Meredith and Assemblyman Pesin were also permitted to ask questions, as were the two attorneys, who submitted their queries in writing to Mr. Ashmead. Although the ACLU accepted this procedure, it later complained that "[the lawyers'] questions were frequently edited by the chairman of the committee."[4]

The hearings contained several major parts. First came Bergel and his witnesses, who spoke in support of his charges. Next came Hauptmann and his witnesses, who angrily dismissed them. Then Bergel appeared in rebuttal, followed by representatives of the administration—Meder, Corwin, and Clothier. After that, the two lawyers, Kaplan and Tauber, summed up their cases.

The hearings opened with Bergel on the stand. In his written statement, he claimed that his political difficulties with Hauptmann

surfaced in the spring of 1933, when he (Bergel) publicly challenged Emil Jordan's benign portrait of Nazi Germany before the
League of Women Voters. The chronology was important, Bergel
argued, because this incident predated all the meetings at which
"the inconsistent reasons for my dismissal, the most grave of which
was incompetence," were discussed. "Professor Hauptmann is
prejudiced against me because I have spoken against the Hitler regime in student meetings," said Bergel. "I am the only member of
the German Department who has done this."

Bergel proceeded to debunk the chairman's academic credentials. He wondered how anyone could produce a Ph.D. dissertation
in five months, and he hinted that Hauptmann had never passed
the *Staatsexamen*. This said, Bergel compared himself favorably to
Emil Jordan, his erstwhile competitor. "Mr. Jordan . . . has his degree in Economics and has never studied either Germanic philology or the technique of teaching," he said. "I have had five years of
University preparation in Germanic philology, under famous spe-
cialists in this field. . . . In addition I have had a year of practice
teaching . . . under careful supervision in the higher schools of
Brieg and Breslau, Germany. I was rated in the best group. . . .
No other member of the German Department has this preparation."

Bergel's most serious charges concerned political indoctrina-
tion in the classroom. "Professor Hauptmann is actively interested
in winning the sympathy [and] admiration of students for the Nazi
system," he said. "Classroom time, legitimately intended for the
study of the German language and literature, has been spent in lectures and discussions concerning the Hitler regime. I state this
from personal observation."

Bergel offered a startling example. In the spring of 1934
he had missed a month of classes while recovering from appendicitis. Hauptmann had taken his place. "The first day after my
return . . . ," he recalled, "Mr. Hauptmann came into the classroom to continue . . . a discussion of German political events. . . .
His two themes were: the lying of American newspapers, and the
beneficial anti-Semitic measures taken by the Hitler movement."
Bergel described the "discussion" as a racist harangue. Hauptmann not only analyzed the permissible levels of "Jewish blood" in

German veins, he also dismissed a question about Thomas Mann's expulsion by saying, "Well, he had a Jewish wife, so they had a right to put him out." Bergel added that many witnesses "will testify to the accuracy of these statements . . . [and] relate . . . more incidents of the same sort."[5]

More than sixty witnesses testified in Bergel's behalf, including eight of his colleagues at N.J.C. Not surprisingly, these faculty members were liberal and anti-Nazi in their beliefs. They described Bergel as a scholar, a "man of broad culture," and "one of the finest professors" at the college. They also portrayed Hauptmann as a bully, an autocrat, and a defender of Hitler's regime. Professor Evalyn Clark declared that "only a person who could agree with [Hauptmann] could be a member of his department." And Professor William Oncken charged that Hauptmann had once "slandered" him by spreading rumors of his incompetence. When challenged by the trustees on this point, Oncken admitted that the man who had told him about these rumors was Bergel.[6]

One of the most respected witnesses was Shirley Smith, a professor of classics at N.J.C. The transcript of Miss Smith's testimony is not in the university archives; the newspaper accounts are not very revealing. However, Miss Smith expressed her feelings about the controversy in a thoughtful letter to the trustees, which is worth quoting. "I have had many chats on many subjects with Professor Hauptmann, often very delightful ones," she wrote,

> [but] the situation in Germany is a subject that I have avoided . . . , feeling that neither of us could talk about it to any good end, so largely emotional are our reactions and so different our conclusions. I realize fully, however, that the position of a member of Mr. Hauptmann's own department who found himself on the other side would be a very difficult one, since the subject could not so easily be avoided.

Miss Smith added: "It would be difficult to convince me that the interests of THE COLLEGE AS A WHOLE . . . are best advanced by having a department think and act as one unit in the regimentation of an army organization. That seems, so far as an outsider can judge, to be the situation in the German Department. . . . Mr. Bergel has not fitted into that close-knit pattern."[7]

The most damaging testimony came from Harold Van Dorn, a political scientist known for his progressive views. Van Dorn said he did not relish his role because he considered Hauptmann a friend and "what I have to say might hurt him." But the facts were obvious—and very important. Hauptmann was devoted to Nazism. He had sent Van Dorn propaganda pamphlets from Germany. He did not believe in "free speech, free press, or freedom to differ." And his prejudice against Bergel was overwhelming. "[Let] me add . . . ," said Van Dorn, "that in an hour's conversation with Professor Hauptmann [about Bergel's dismissal] not once was incompetence mentioned as a reason . . . and not once was economy mentioned. It was a confidential conversation and therefore I cannot go further."[8]

In the following days and weeks, dozens of students came forward to testify for Bergel. Their sheer numbers and heartfelt enthusiasm can hardly be exaggerated. They described Bergel again and again as "a fine teacher" and "an outstanding professor." What is interesting, however, is that these students were often enthusiastic about Hauptmann's teaching, while the students who would testify later for Hauptmann were extremely critical of Bergel's classroom performance. Some of Bergel's witnesses portrayed the chairman as dogmatic and domineering, but the clear majority considered him competent, friendly, and genuinely interested in their welfare.

A number of witnesses accused Hauptmann of spreading pro-Nazi propaganda. One student said he brought newspapers into class to refute the "lies" about Germany and to explain the wonderful things that were happening there. Another claimed that Hauptmann had praised Hitler's intention to "put women back into the home." A third witness, who had done secretarial work for the chairman, said he once dictated a letter to Nazi Propaganda Minister Joseph Goebbels, asking for information on German art and culture. The letter was never finished or sent, she added, because Hauptmann forgot about it and she destroyed the notes.[9]

Some of the charges made big headlines. One witness "created a sensation" by alleging that Hauptmann had fired a book at her head. But none of her classmates could remember the incident. A few days later, a former student of Hauptmann charged that he had turned her into a Nazi sympathizer during her years at N.J.C. Visibly upset, she claimed, among other things, that Hauptmann had referred to Woodrow Wilson as a *Schweinehund*. Oddly, however, the woman could not recall the class where the remark was made, and would not name any of the students who were present at the time.[10]

One of Bergel's witnesses, Mary Atwood, lived in the campus German House. (Virtually everyone else there would testify for Hauptmann.) Miss Atwood said that most of her fellow residents were "pro-Nazi" because Professor Hauptmann "is very persuasive, and can talk most anybody into thinking most anything." Her testimony was severely challenged by the trustees, who treated her with suspicion and disrespect. Their questions and comments included: "All right, now what do you want to say?" "Is that really of any importance?" "Please come to the point." "Have you spoken with Dr. Bergel?" (No.) "Are you a member of the National Student League?" (No, again.) The examination of Miss Atwood spoke volumes about the outlook of the trustees.[11]

Approximately half of the students and alumni who testified for Bergel were Jewish. They spoke freely about alleged anti-Semitism in the German Department, and their remarks were fairly consistent. One witness said Hauptmann had complained that Jews "were dominating [Germany] through control of finances." Another claimed he had "condoned" Nazi anti-Semitism in a private conversation with her. But these were minority opinions. On the whole, the Bergel witnesses viewed Hauptmann as fair and friendly to Jewish students. A few of them recalled that he had criticized Hitler's anti-Semitic policies in class. And no one could remember Hauptmann's remarks, described by Bergel, about Thomas Mann's expulsion or the permissible level of Jewish blood in German veins.[12]

University officials received a number of letters on this issue. Almost all supported Hauptmann. As one man, a Jewish immigrant, wrote Dean Corwin:

I was astonished to read in the papers about [Hauptmann's] antisemitic tendencies. I remember very well when he was over in Germany in 1934/35 and studied at the university of my home-town that he sometimes talked to my father about the methods used against the Jews in a detesting manner. At that time already he offered my father his help to bring my brother over to this country, and later when we both decided to go to U.S.A. he was always very helpful. We got our first affidavit from him, and when he was not able to complete it he provided us with another one from one of his Jewish friends.[13]

Hauptmann spent almost five full days on the witness stand. He began by reading a statement that defended his own conduct and justified Bergel's dismissal. Not surprisingly, he portrayed himself as a demanding yet compassionate man who had tried to work with Bergel, who had extended his contract, and who had attempted to find him jobs at other colleges. In Bergel's first year at N.J.C., Hauptmann stated, there had been complaints about his teaching. He had defended Bergel, however, "feeling that he must be given a chance to accustom himself to new conditions and to make good. He was reappointed for 1932/33; the complaints continued; I twice spoke to Mr. Bergel about them. He answered in an arrogant manner."[14]

At the end of the year, Hauptmann continued, he had gone through the examination papers of all the beginners' sections in German. He discovered that "Mr. Bergel's students were less well grounded than those in any other section, and . . . that his grades were disproportionately high." Hauptmann brought this to the attention of Acting Dean Meder, who decided that Bergel should be dismissed with one year's notice. However, "as [Bergel] was without other means, and in grief because of the loss of a child to which Mrs. Bergel had just given birth, I suggested that the one year's notice be extended to two years. Accordingly, at the close of the college year 1932–33, I told Mr. Bergel that his services would not be required after June 1935, that he had better look around for another [position], and that I should be glad to help him."[15]

Hauptmann had other grievances as well. He claimed that Bergel had broken a promise to live in the New Brunswick area, moving instead to Cranford, where he was difficult to reach. He said that Bergel showed no interest in the German Club, the German House, or the German table in the dining room; that he rarely kept office hours; that he attended only one faculty meeting in three years. "There were open complaints from the other instructors," said Hauptmann, ". . . that while they had to sacrifice themselves for the good of the college, Mr. Bergel abstained completely from any such duty." [16]

Hauptmann turned next to the charges that had been leveled against him. He denied that he had ever "slandered" Professor Oncken, or thrown a book at a student, or called Woodrow Wilson a *Schweinehund*. He insisted that he had passed the *Staatsexamen*. He dismissed the allegations of anti-Semitism by noting that a Jewish woman had tutored his children and lived in his home; that his former landlady was Jewish and "today we are good friends"; that he had hired a Jew, Ruth Wagner, to replace him while he was on leave; and that his relations with Jewish students were always above reproach. As for the charges by Professor Van Dorn, Hauptmann claimed that their "one hour" conversation about Bergel had lasted for ten minutes, with Van Dorn doing the talking. He added: "It is true that I [gave] the Political Science Department . . . a number of books and pamphlets in order to support [the effort] to keep an impartial view of the German situation. . . . I asked Professor Van Dorn whether he wanted such material. He said that he did. . . . I am astonished that [he] . . . now turns around and accuses me of injecting propaganda into his department." [17]

Hauptmann's testimony was uneventful, and the trustees did not press him very hard. The tough questions came from Bergel's attorney, who submitted them in writing to Chairman Ashmead, and from Assemblyman Pesin, who had sponsored New Jersey's "Anti-Nazi Law." Their questions focused on Hauptmann's views about Germany, anti-Semitism, and Bergel himself.

Hauptmann did not try to hide his admiration for the "New Germany." As the committee's final report noted: "In the rise of Hitler he saw the possibility of moulding the German people into a united nation. [His] hope in this regard is so strong that he is disposed to overlook . . . the general policies of Hitler . . . and to discount many of the reports published in American newspapers concerning conditions and events in Germany. He believes that the overwhelming majority of the German people are behind Hitler and has great faith in the ability of the German people to solve their own problems."[18]

In this public forum, at least, Hauptmann refused to condemn Hitler's treatment of the Jews. He explained the rise of anti-Semitism by noting that Germany had economic problems, and that the influx of Polish Jews had made things worse. When asked, specifically, for his opinion of Nazi anti-Semitism, he replied: "I have no belief in that matter at all." When asked, "How far can you go in the direction of anti-Semitism?" he said: "I would go about as far as . . . the United States [goes] in excluding the Japanese people. It is up to every government to . . . decide what should be done about it."[19]

The most telling questions concerned Hauptmann's feelings about Bergel. In his personal statement, the chairman described himself as a judicious man, incapable of holding a grudge. In his testimony, however, he revealed his prejudice in no uncertain terms. At one point, he claimed that he had *never* heard a student praise Bergel's teaching—a rather remarkable statement in light of the campus petitions and the dozens of students who had spoken at the hearings. At another point, Hauptmann expressed his disgust at Bergel's constant criticism of the Nazi government. In what may have been the most revealing single sentence of his testimony, he said: "I cannot have any respect for any man who besmirches the country where he was born."[20]

Alice Schlimbach and Emil Jordan followed Hauptmann to the stand. Miss Schlimbach's testimony was almost comically inept. She listed every imaginable flaw in Bergel's personality, character, and appearance, including the fact that he did not look mature enough to be a good teacher. Assemblyman Pesin asked whether Bergel should grow a beard. "It would take more than whiskers to give [him] dignity," she replied. Miss Schlimbach also had a "feeling" that Bergel was a Communist. The feeling was based on "woman's intuition," which she seemed to prefer over evidence or first-hand knowledge.[21]

Jordan's testimony was similar, but far less amusing. He began by characterizing Bergel's faculty supporters as "left-wingers" who advocated such "radical measures" as a teachers' union and the right to strike. He then accused the Bergels, who had been his social companions for several years, of remarkable ingratitude to Friedrich Hauptmann. When Miss Cook "came to our department . . . and told [Hauptmann] . . . that her fiance was living in Germany and that they could not get married, he at once took steps to help these two young people. . . . I have often heard Mr. and Mrs. Bergel say . . . that they owed their American start to nobody but Dr. Hauptmann. But apparently they have forgotten that now and are very indignant that Dr. Hauptmann is not guaranteeing them an annual income for the rest of their lives."[22]

Jordan also criticized Bergel's "complete divorcement" from his department and his college. He supported Hauptmann's and Schlimbach's testimony that Bergel "couldn't be bothered with routine matters" like department meetings, faculty meetings, social functions, and extracurricular activities. "I would have welcomed Mr. Bergel's cooperation," he added, "but it never came."[23]

Hauptmann's student witnesses echoed these views. Many of them were German-Americans living in the campus German House. Their written statements to the committee were very similar: they praised Hauptmann and Schlimbach as wonderful role models and excellent teachers; they condemned Bergel for ignoring their scholarly and cultural interests. These students denied that pro-Nazi propaganda had been disseminated in their classes or in the German House. Several of them said that the Horst Wessel song, the Nazi anthem, had been sung in fun at the German House, but that Schlimbach had found out about it and ordered them to stop. One student admitted, rather proudly, that she had a framed etching of Adolf Hitler in her room. She explained: "I like him as a dictator and a man."[24]

Hauptmann's supporters were disturbed by the charges and furious at the people who made them. Many believed there was a conspiracy to defame him. One witness blamed "a few [Jews] from the National Student League." Another spoke of an "organized Jewish anti-Nazi movement" on campus." Still another said the students opposing Hauptmann "were of the Jewish race." She added: "I know the Jews are quite touchy where the anti-Semitism question is concerned and perhaps they . . . misconstrued some statements in regard to Germany."[25]

Only one Jewish student, Evelyn Lehman, testified for Hauptmann. She lived in the German House, liked it there, and could remember no examples of pro-Nazi or anti-Semitic propaganda. In fact, she said, "I have never heard of any German faculty member with the exception of Mr. Bergel mention his own views of [the Hitler government.]"[26]

Miss Lehman also contended that other Jewish students wanted to testify for Hauptmann but were afraid to do so. She suspected that peer pressure and concern about employment prospects were responsible for this faintheartedness. Miss Lehman did not mention any names, but there is some evidence to back up her remarks. In the files of the Ashmead committee, for example, is a notarized letter from a student who took six courses from Hauptmann and two from Bergel. It reads: "I cannot appear personally to render this testimony and I do not wish my name published in connection with this investigation. . . . There was no Nazi propaganda in any class that I attended. Since I am of the Jewish faith, I certainly would have been the first to recognize anything in the German Department that might have been construed as Nazi propaganda."[27]

On June 21 Bergel's attorney sent a "confidential" note to the trustees committee. "Would it be considered in order," wrote Sidney Kaplan, "for me to make a suggestion for an amicable compromise and settlement of this controversy [in] the best interest of all concerned, the college, Dr. Hauptmann, the German faculty, Dr. Bergel, and the interested public?"[28]

The terms of Kaplan's "compromise" were astonishing. They represented, quite simply, a flag of surrender by Lienhard Bergel. The major points were:

(1) Dr. Bergel to withdraw all charges against the administration and the German faculty.

(2) The German faculty to withdraw all charges against Dr. Bergel.

(3) The college to reaffirm the position taken in Dr. Clothier's letter that no charges have been brought against Dr. Bergel.

(4) Dr. Bergel to be reappointed for one year at the end of which the college may fail to reappoint him without any question or complaint from Dr. Bergel.

The "compromise" was signed by Kaplan and Bergel. Why did they agree to these terms? Why did they withdraw their serious charges against the University in order to gain one more year of employment for Bergel at N.J.C.? There are no conclusive answers, but some points are clear. For one thing, Kaplan was tired of the case. He had been working on it for a month and wanted to move on to something else. For another, Bergel was now unemployed, and had a wife and a baby to support. His savings were minimal. The extra year would allow him to bring home a pay check while he looked for other work. Finally, the two men must have understood that Bergel would not be vindicated. Many witnesses had praised him, but others had not. His entire department had condemned his behavior. He still faced a withering cross-examination from the trustees, as well as the destructive testimony of Meder, Corwin, and Clothier. The time had come to throw in the towel.

The other question, of course, is: why didn't the trustees accept this compromise? There are two likely answers. The first is that the trustees were determined to see this process to the end. They wanted to cross-examine Bergel, and they wanted university officials to dispute his allegations in a public forum. The second answer, the more probable one, is that the trustees could not get the American Civil Liberties Union to agree to a vital part of the compromise. This point was made clearly in a letter to Chairman Ashmead by an ACLU official. She wrote:

You ask if the [ACLU] "is willing to make a statement that the discharge of Mr. Bergel was not for political reasons and, further, that there has been no Nazi propaganda on the campus of [N.J.C.]." Any statement that the [ACLU] makes on this case must be based upon the reports of our representatives at the . . . Trustee hearings and only after the [ACLU] has given full consideration to those reports. It is, therefore, impossible, for us to reach any conclusions until the hearings are closed.[29]

Without the ACLU's full and immediate cooperation, the trustees were not about to end the hearings.

The investigation continued. On July 12 the *Daily Home News* headline read: "Severe Examination in Store for Bergel." The headline was prophetic. The trustees grilled Bergel for several days; his testimony ran to more than four-hundred pages. His main contention once again was that he had been discharged for political reasons—his "unwillingness to cooperate in [disseminating] emotional Nazi propaganda."[30]

Bergel now claimed that he had told Acting Dean Meder about his "political problems" in their meeting of September 1933. "I said [to Meder], 'I am not fortunate enough to share the political views of Professor Hauptmann, and I believe there is something that might point to the motive of [the] decision [to dismiss me.]'" The trustees did not believe him. For one thing, Meder had denied this; for another, Bergel's ally, Professor William Braun of Barnard, had made no mention of "political problems" when he wrote Meder in October 1933 about Bergel's "misgivings as to the security of his position." On this vital point, Bergel was on very weak ground.[31]

The trustees questioned Bergel about his failure to attend routine meetings and his apparent disinterest in crucial department activities. Bergel's answers did not impress them. He was not active in the German Club, he said, because Miss Schlimbach, "the central figure," was prejudiced against him. He stayed away from the German House because it was "the center of Nazi propaganda in my opinion—I am not critical of the institution itself." And he did not attend faculty meetings when he first arrived at N.J.C. because Hauptmann had told him they were boring and unimportant.[32]

Ashmead pressed him hard on this issue. He asked: "Now, you attended some meetings [after that?"] Bergel said yes.

Ashmead. And what was your attitude as derived from your observation?

Bergel. Well, it was not so boring as I thought. . . . Those meetings that I attended were worth while.

Ashmead had the answer he wanted. He asked: "What was the date of the last faculty meeting that you attended?"

Bergel. I have a very bad memory for dates.

Ashmead. Have you attended any this year?

Bergel. I don't think so.

Ashmead. Do you remember whether you attended any last year?

Bergel. I think so.

Ashmead. How many?

Bergel. Well, it can be one or two.[33]

Here was Bergel's greatest weakness—his failure to do the routine things that were expected of a faculty member at N.J.C. And a fair number of students, including some who chose not to testify, were aware of the problem. One recent graduate wrote President Clothier that "I cannot remember seeing Mr. Bergel at but one German Club meeting. . . . In fact, I rarely saw [him] except between classes in the Annex and his days in the dining room. He was very seldom at his desk in the office." And another alumnus wrote Ashmead that "Mr. Bergel did not cooperate in any way for the benefit of the activities of the German Department."[34]

The trustees were also offended by Bergel's demeanor. He struck them as a man with a superiority complex, who flaunted his academic credentials while viewing his colleagues with contempt. Ashmead did not have much trouble making this point.

Ashmead. Now when was it you discovered that you were the best professor in the German Department?

Bergel. I discovered it quite early, that I had the normal preparation—I had assumed that the other teachers would have the same preparation.

Ashmead.   And what was the date that you discovered that?

Bergel.   That was also within the first few weeks.

Ashmead.   You were still 26 years old? [35]

Bergel realized his mistake. He tried to backtrack—"I never said I was the best teacher in the German Department"—but Ashmead had him trapped.

Ashmead.   Well, when did you come to the conclusion that there was no one around the college to whom you could talk about subjects you were interested in; you did say that?

Bergel.   I said only in my department, however, not other departments. . . . I found that [my colleagues] were not able to discuss those questions which are customary to be discussed among colleagues of a professional nature. [36]

Bergel was probably correct. He *was* the only "intellectual" in his department. He had different tastes and different interests. But in making these statements, he reinforced the impression that he would be better off teaching somewhere else.

The final testimony of the hearings came from the major university officials, Corwin, Meder, and Clothier. All read prepared statements. Corwin and Meder discussed the nuts-and-bolts of the case: the three-year rule, the severe budget cuts, the decline in enrollments. Corwin denied that she had ever threatened to withhold written recommendations for Bergel in the event he contested his dismissal. Meder denied that Bergel had ever raised the issue of "political discrimination" in 1933, or that he had not been given adequate reasons for his discharge. Meder also took a mean-spirited swing at Mrs. Bergel, who had openly criticized the quality of instruction in the German department. "It is a recognized policy in college administration," he said, "that in engaging a man consideration is to be given also to the personality of his wife. We felt that the situation in this instance was such that there might be a lack of harmony in the department." [37]

Clothier's testimony was the most damaging of all. The president stressed three basic points. First, Bergel had not demonstrated the "outstanding personal qualities" or the "outstanding qualities of a classroom teacher" which "we desire in persons . . . promoted to assistant professor." Second, Bergel had been "poorly advised in approaching persons outside the University to interest themselves in his behalf before appealing to the president of the institution." (Clothier really meant that Bergel had been disloyal, but he did not use that term.) Third, Rutgers had firmly adhered to the principles of academic freedom and free speech. "Until this controversy developed," he said, "no intimation had ever been made to me that [these principles were violated] in any degree whatever, in any department in the University. Nor has there been evidence that un-American principles have been advocated in any department or by any faculty member."[38]

Neither attorney made a formal summation, but Sidney Kaplan urged the trustees to include six findings in their report. The most important were: that Bergel was "competent and efficient"; that he was qualified for promotion; that Hauptmann's judgment was the main factor in the administration's decision to dismiss Bergel; and that political differences were the "principal factor" in Hauptmann's judgment.[39]

Then it was Fred Tauber's turn. He looked at Kaplan and said, "I formally deny any and all allegations contained in Mr. Bergel's charge." The hearings were over.[40]

The trustees promised a "prompt decision." They were true to their word. On August 18, less than a month after the final session, the report was released to the press. There had been no disagreements among the members, no dissenting opinions.

The report painted a rosy picture of life at N.J.C. The College was "nobly conceived [and] loyally supported" by the students, teachers, alumni, trustees, and residents of New Jersey. Everyone got along well. "Members of the faculty of various religious affiliation and political background have worked together in splendid harmony."[41]

The report commended Hauptmann for "the remarkable development of the German Department under his supervision and the reported efficiency of the students who have majored in German." It described him as "a capable organizer," "a very efficient teacher," and "a man of the highest ideals, untiring in his devotion to his work." It found no evidence that he was anti-Semitic or that he had disseminated Nazi propaganda in his classes. In fact, the report added, "the Committee finds that none of the classrooms of Professor Hauptmann, Miss Schlimbach, Dr. Jordan, or Mrs. Hauptmann was ever used for the purpose of spreading pro-Nazi propaganda and this statement is equally true, obviously, of Mr. Bergel's classes." [42]

The report also cleared Hauptmann of distributing propaganda on the campus. It claimed that the pamphlets he had sent to Professor Van Dorn were not "improper" for use in political science courses, and that, in any event, the decision to use them was made by Van Dorn. As for the Campbell pamphlets, the report accepted Hauptmann's explanation that he had left them accidentally on Bergel's desk without even reading the contents. Rather remarkably, the report criticized *Bergel* for allowing students to take the pamphlets and for mailing copies to prominent state officials. [43]

The committee's praise for Hauptmann was matched only by its disdain for his accuser. The report did not challenge Bergel's competence. In fact, it called him "amply qualified in the knowledge of his subject." But the report did question his usefulness as a teacher, his unwillingness to take suggestions, his arrogance as a colleague, his disinterest in extra-curricular activities, and even his scholarly pretensions. "Mr. Bergel is very much interested in books," it said. "However, there is no evidence that any creative scholarship on his part has been brought to fruition." [44]

The report then confronted the central charge: that Hauptmann had decided to fire Bergel for political reasons, and that University officials had rubber-stamped this decision without independent investigation. "The fact is that Professor Hauptmann did not make the decision," the report concluded. "The committee is of the opinion that Acting Dean Meder, Dean Corwin, and Dr. Clothier each gave Mr. Bergel's case very thorough and careful consideration before they made their respective decisions." Therefore, "the committee affirms each of the decisions of [these officials] not to approve the reappointment of Mr. Bergel after the conclusion of his contract on June 30, 1935." [45]

The final report—or Ashmead report—was a predictable document. The authors were determined to protect their University, which was really on trial. To do so they defended Friedrich Hauptmann, accepted his stories, believed his witnesses, and praised him and his department in rather inflated terms. But the trustees acted for another reason as well: they believed that the basic charges brought by Lienhard Bergel were untrue. They did not think he deserved promotion, and they did not trust his supporters, who seemed to be left-wingers, troublemakers, and disgruntled Jews. The trustees had done a thankless and thorough job—that could not be denied—but their conclusions had been marred by their prejudices, although on this score they were hardly alone.

7 THE AFTERMATH

On August 20, 1935, President Clothier left New Brunswick for his summer home in Nova Scotia. Weary but relieved, he made sure that copies of the Ashmead report had been mailed to Governor Harold Hoffman, to all state legislators, to dozens of newspapers, and to the trustees, regents, and important alumni of the University. In addition, he sent a personal note to each faculty witness who had backed the administration at the hearings. To Friedrich and Marie Hauptmann, he wrote: "We all appreciate what an extremely trying experience this investigation was . . . and I wish to . . . congratulate you . . . upon the splendid spirit which you both showed throughout the episode."[1]

In reality the "episode" was far from over. Letters and telegrams poured into Clothier's office. Most were complimentary; some were critical; a few were bizarre. One legislator applauded "the calm and diligent manner in which the committee conducted its proceedings." Another assured Clothier that "the senator from Cape May County is back of [you]." Various letters described the Ashmead report as "masterly," "unassailable," and "just about perfect." From New York City, philanthropist August Heckscher wrote Clothier: "The dropping of Dr. Bergel was justified . . . from the angle of necessary economies. . . . Rutgers has done more than its share in this painstaking investigation. . . . You ought to proceed to [other matters]."[2]

There were dissenters, of course. "I have been deeply shocked by the clean bill of health conferred on Dr. Hauptmann by the investigating committee," an alumnus wrote Clothier. "In protest . . . I am taking steps to cancel my class insurance which I took out in 1923." Another complained: "I do not believe an American institution has the right to harbor a man . . . who favors rule by beasts. . . . Let him go back to Germany. He has no place in my alma mater."[3]

The newspaper editorials generally supported the trustees. The *Daily Home News*, which had followed the hearings carefully, agreed that Bergel's dismissal was "logical," given the declining enrollments in German at N.J.C. "Since Mr. Bergel was the last to be hired," it said, "he might naturally be designated as the one to go." The *Jersey Journal* was more reserved in its opinion, although it praised the committee members for their devotion to duty. "This has been the busiest and unpleasantest summer for the trustees of Rutgers . . . in many a long year . . . [They] have done well to manage to preserve an air of decorum, in spite of the hurlyburly possibilities of the situation."[4]

As expected, the German-American newspapers split along political lines. The pro-Nazi *Deutscher-Weckruf* urged university officials to "render an apology to Dr. Hauptmann . . . [and] compensate him in an appropriate manner." But the anti-Nazi *Neue Volks-Zeitung* believed that the only compensation Hauptmann deserved was a one-way ticket back to Germany. "A real Nazi," it teased, "should instruct only pure Aryan children—if there is such a thing!—and should regard it as beneath his dignity to teach Jews." In between these positions stood the *Staatszeitung und Herold*, which probably spoke for the majority of German-Americans on this issue. The newspaper reported the trustees' findings solemnly, without jubilation or regret. It seemed embarrassed by the whole affair and relieved to see it end.[5]

Most of the criticism of the report came from predictable sources. Attorney Sidney J. Kaplan called the findings a "whitewash" and a "disgrace to the University." The state American Legion demanded an investigation of "alien professors" in New Brunswick, while Assemblyman Samuel Pesin compared the German Department to a Nazi colony. "Hauptmann went far beyond his right to hold certain political views," Pesin declared: "He [used] his position in an American university to defend and promote the political ideas of a foreign government, which are directly contrary to the basic ideals of democracy."[6]

The ACLU also tore into the Ashmead report, although it differed from Pesin and the Legion on one important point. Its position, understandably, was that Hauptmann had a right to promote his political opinions, but no right "to drive a man of contrary views from the faculty." The ACLU's twenty-page report written by Ellen Donahue, reached four major conclusions: Bergel was a competent teacher; Hauptmann was clearly pro-Nazi; Bergel was clearly anti-Nazi; and Hauptmann showed "definite prejudice against Bergel on account of their political differences."[7]

In a letter to the Rutgers trustees, the ACLU described the Bergel hearings as the "most searching and . . . lengthy public inquiry of its sort in academic history." Still, the letter urged the trustees to reject the Ashmead report and to reinstate Bergel at once. Failure to do so, it went on, would "regretfully oblige" the ACLU to "take the issue" to the New Jersey Legislature.[8]

Within days, however, the ACLU changed its position. The main reason, without question, was the pressure applied by the pro-Bergel forces in New Brunswick. In October 1935 Professors Clark, West, and Van Dorn invited Ellen Donahue to Rutgers for a "discussion." They warned her that a Nazi-hunt could easily turn into a Red-hunt, with themselves as the victims. The following day, Ms. Donahue wrote to Roger Baldwin, the ACLU's executive director: "[These people] think a legislative investigation would be a tragedy . . . [and] result in many dismissals, for they are all considered radicals. . . . Mr. Pesin, and his kind, they recognize as no advocates of Free Speech."[9]

Baldwin also received some remarkable advice from Alan Silver, the young radical at Rutgers. (Baldwin was impressed enough to reply at length.) In his letter, Silver claimed that a legislative probe would surely get around to "un-American activities" in New Brunswick. And President Clothier would no doubt convince the "dumb legislators" that Bergel's case had been trumped up by left-wing groups like the National Student League. This would not only damage Bergel, it would also "jeopardize the position of students and teachers in the liberal and radical camps." Put simply, the remedy was not worth the risk.

Silver offered some additional advice. "The NSL believes that we should all confine investigation efforts to the [American

Association of University Professors]. Also . . . by hook or by crook, another position be got for Mr. Bergel. . . . These two items might not be so spectacular, but at least we would know we were going in the right direction." [10]

In 1935 the AAUP was a rather weak and timid organization. It rarely challenged politicians or college administrators on non-economic issues. Although the AAUP had a Committee on Academic Freedom, it did not aggressively pursue cases involving the harassment or dismissal of political dissidents. Its main concerns in the Depression were salary cuts and working conditions, not the protection of individual rights. [11]

The AAUP chapter at Rutgers, formed in 1922, had seventy-five members, including Evalyn Clark, Harold Van Dorn, Selman Waksman, and Miriam West. Friedrich Hauptmann and Albert Meder were also members. Lienhard Bergel was not. [12]

Nevertheless, Bergel had contacted the AAUP's national office when the hearings opened in May. After listing his own grievances, he claimed that an AAUP investigation "into conditions in general at [N.J.C.] would reveal cases of arbitrary strong-arm decisions . . . in departments other than German." But no one at the AAUP seemed to care. "Let's not have any fight . . . unless we get dragged into it," said one official. "All my past experience with [N.J.C.] leads me to feel that our intervention [would] be a time-wasting futility." [13]

When the hearings ended, Ellen Donahue sent a copy of her report to the AAUP in Washington. The response was predictable. No one lifted a finger for Bergel. The internal memos from AAUP headquarters all said the same thing: "I doubt the need of any action . . . put the [ACLU] report in our Rutgers file." Or: "I . . . doubt whether [we] should take any action . . . recommend filing this material for information." As one memo put it, "The [Rutgers] trustees interpret evidence one way and the [ALCU] interprets it another way." Why get caught in the middle? [14]

The big loser in this withdrawal from responsibility was Lienhard Bergel, now unemployed. In October 1935 he wrote Alan Silver about his plight. He wanted the AAUP to help him, he said, but he did not want to approach them alone. "I feel . . . it would be preferable if the Civil Liberties Union . . . brought the matter to their attention. Do you think it would be possible to arrange a conference between members of the [ACLU] and me, in which this question might be discussed?" There is no record that a conference ever took place; the papers of the ACLU do not mention one. But a few weeks later, an official of the ACLU did urge the AAUP to begin a formal probe of the Bergel case. "We understand that members of the [Rutgers] faculty as well as students are anxious for the support of outside groups," wrote Lucille Milner of the ACLU's Committee on Academic Freedom. "An investigation by the [AAUP] would be extremely helpful." [15]

Nothing happened. The AAUP responded that its "legal advisor" had "deemed it inexpedient [to investigate] the Bergel matter, in view of the complications involved." This empty explanation did not sit well with Milner, who suspected an ulterior motive. Her testy reply ended with a question: "Is Dr. Hauptmann still the head of [your] unit at the college?" [16]

The answer was no. The following day, an AAUP vice-president sent Milner a list of the association's officers in New Brunswick. "I wonder what could have given you the impression that Dr. Hauptmann was one of them," he sniped. "I shall place your letter in the Rutgers file in case there should be occasion to give the institution further attention." [17]

That ended the correspondence. There would be no "further attention" paid to Rutgers or to Bergel. The AAUP did not mention him again.

On October 11, 1935, the Rutgers trustees accepted the Ashmead report at their fall meeting in New Brunswick. The vote was unanimous. The trustees also approved the promotion of Emil Jordan to the rank of assistant professor. Jordan had just become an American citizen, a matter of no small importance to the Rutgers administration. As Dean Corwin told him: "I am delighted. . . . In view of all the excitement started by the American Legion, it [is] helpful to have this matter all settled." [18]

A month later, Corwin settled another ticklish matter: the

future of Marie Hauptmann. Noting that the trustees "have expressed themselves as opposed to the general policy of having both husband and wife on the faculty," she told Friedrich Hauptmann that his wife would have to give up her assistantship by June of 1937.* In order to cushion the blow, however, Corwin promised Hauptmann some compensation in the future. "It is our hope," she wrote him, "that we may . . . be able to make an increase in your salary which would make the consequent adjustment in your family budget less difficult."[19]

By this time, organized support for Bergel had all but disappeared. The American Legion had run out of rhetoric; the ACLU had run out of ideas; the AAUP had simply run away. The key remaining supporters, as usual, were Alan Silver and the National Student League. In September Silver tried to revive interest in the Bergel case by holding a mass rally in New Brunswick. He had approached the ACLU about a "speaker with a national reputation," someone like Heywood Broun or Harry F. Ward. "We need about 7 days of advance for publicity," he wrote Lucille Milner. "Given a well-known speaker, 1,000 turnout is assured."[20]

The rally never took place. The ACLU did not produce a well-known speaker, and the Bergel case could no longer generate much enthusiasm by itself. Many of Bergel's supporters had graduated in

---

* According to Alan Silver, Rutgers had a nepotism rule when Mrs. Hauptmann was on the faculty. "There was a longstanding . . . rule against husband and wife being on the University faculty at the same time," he writes. "[Mrs. Hauptmann] was an obvious case of the kind of nepotism which the University rule was designed to forbid. The administration carefully concealed this violation . . . during the 1935 hearings." (See, *Daily Targum*, January 21, 1987; also Silver's unpublished paper, "The Economic and Administrative Considerations in the Bergel Case," in Rutgers University Archives.) Silver asserts that Mrs. Hauptmann alone was allowed to work in violation of this nepotism rule until 1937, when embarrassed Rutgers authorities ended her employment at N.J.C. In fact, Silver's assertion is incorrect. Rutgers did not have a nepotism rule—written or unwritten—at this time. On the contrary, there were *numerous* instances of husbands and wives working together on the university faculty. (See, for example, the personnel files of Virginia Sedmen, Millie McCoy, Mary Olney, and Mrs. Eva Oncken.) Mrs. Hauptmann's case was hardly exceptional, although, in the end, it may have forced the trustees to take a stand on the nepotism issue.

June. Others saw no hope, and some danger, in opposing the will of administrators and trustees. "We were thoroughly beaten," a student leader recalled. "The case was over. There was nothing more to do." [21]

There would still be sporadic meetings on the issue, organized largely by radical groups. But they were poorly attended, and Bergel himself began to stay away. According to Ellen Donahue, "He does not want to be considered a radical and fears ruin if he is supported by Communists." On another occasion, she wrote: "Poor Bergel . . . is so frightened . . . he'll be mistaken for a 'red.'" [22]

In late September Bergel's remaining supporters formed the NJC Committee for Academic Freedom. With perhaps three dozen members, many from the NSL, it proved remarkably adept at generating press coverage for rallies that almost no one attended. Headlines such as "Bergel Protest Movement Grows" and "NJC Grads Plan Meeting to Aid Bergel" were quite common in the fall of 1935. These headlines appeared to worry Dean Corwin; she even sent an aide to take notes at one such rally in Newark. The notes read, in part: "35 present; vast majority Jewish; Meeting orderly. . . . Apparently little money. . . . [One member] asked that great care be taken not to imply general alumni support. [The chairman] professed concern when told that many alumni objected." [23]

The group held four or five meetings. In December it condemned the "growing wave of reaction" in America and called for the "immediate and unqualified reinstatement of Mr. Bergel to his position as an instructor at N.J.C." This done, the committee disbanded, leaving Bergel entirely on his own.

What did he do in the months following his departure from N.J.C.? The answer is unclear. Late in 1935 a reporter interviewed him for a human-interest story in the *New Brunswick Sunday Times*. "With his wife and small son," he wrote, "Mr. Bergel is staying at the home of Mrs. Bergel's mother in Cranford. . . . They are living on their savings. . . . Despite his lack of employment, [Bergel] finds his time well-filled . . . with the research work in linguistics in which he is greatly interested." [24]

In 1985, however, Dr. Bergel gave a very different version of his life in these trying times. In a taped interview he claimed to have been on the payroll of the FBI. The day after the hearings ended, he recalled:

> A person came to our house and identified himself as an FBI agent. [He said] 'I come . . . to ask . . . whether you . . . are willing to work for us. We need someone whose German is fresh . . . on whom we can rely. . . .' And so I received my identification tag and also a secret FBI telephone number. . . . I worked . . . probably five days a week. There was an enormous amount of paper, of material they had there. . . . I just had to translate documents and to interpret passages.

Bergel continued his remarkable story:

Question.   You were paid by the FBI?

Mr. Bergel. That was my main income. That started immediately, the day after my dismissal.

Question.   Do you have any written documentation on that?

Mr. Bergel. No, perhaps I purposely did not keep that so it would not fall in the wrong hands.

Question.   Did you meet with other FBI agents?

Mr. Bergel. Oh, there were quite a few of them, about five six.

Question.   Did you go to an office to meet them?

Mr. Bergel. Oh, yes.

Question.   Where was the office? Do you remember?

Mr. Bergel. I racked my brain where it was. I cannot tell you where it was.[25]

There is no available evidence to support Bergel's story. His FBI file does not mention any employment with the Bureau. And he apparently told no one about this job, not even his wife. During his interview in 1985, Mrs. Bergel sat by his side. She did not attempt to refute his story, but several months later, after reviewing the tape with Alan Silver, she wrote our committee that "I remember nothing of the FBI job."[26]

It seems clear, in fact, that Bergel was unemployed and virtually penniless during this period. In October 1935 he wrote to

Ellen Donahue about his inability to get some material that he had left at Rutgers. "Since I am unemployed," he said, "I have to be extremely economical with traveling expenses, otherwise I would have gone to New Brunswick myself." The following month a group of Bergel's supporters discussed the problem of finding him a job. The group—and Bergel—agreed that a "tour which would send [him] to lecture on Nazi issues" had great appeal. The tour never materialized, though Bergel gave a number of lectures in 1936 on "the meaning of Nazism." His talk at the Jewish Community Center in New Brunswick drew a standing-room-only crowd. It was sponsored by the American League Against War and Fascism, a well-known Communist front.[27]

In 1936 Mrs. Bergel obtained a teaching job at the Kent Place School in Summit, New Jersey. This was very important, for the Bergels had used up their modest savings and were then on home relief. Their biggest problem, of course, was Bergel's failure to land a permanent position, a problem compounded by the need for recommendations from Rutgers. In April 1936, for example, the president of the City College of New York wrote to Clothier about Bergel's credentials:

> Of course, I read in the papers about the long argument that was precipitated when his appointment at the College for Women was not renewed. Will you please let me have your frank opinion concerning: (a) his general scholarship and his authority in the field of German, (b) his effectiveness as a teacher, and (c) his personality, character and general dependability.[28]

Clothier replied by telephone. His words were carefully measured and hardly effusive. He told President Robinson that "so far as I know, [Bergel's] knowledge of his subject is adequate and that he is a good teacher, although I have never heard that he is an outstanding one and I thought he was poorly advised in the attitude which he had taken when an instructor at Rutgers." Clothier added: "I made the one recommendation that if [Robinson] does engage Mr. Bergel . . . he do so for a definite term at first rather than on a continuing appointment."[29]

This was not the worst of it. A few weeks later the headmaster at The Hotchkiss School wrote to Hauptmann about Bergel's qualifications. (The headmaster apparently knew nothing about the Bergel-Hauptmann affair.) "We are looking for a first-rate man to teach German and Latin," he stated. "We have an application from Mr. Lienhard Bergel, who says . . . he was a member of [your] German Department. . . . I should appreciate a frank letter from you giving your impression of his personality and character and your estimate of his ability."[30]

Hauptmann gave the letter to Dean Corwin. She responded by sending the headmaster a copy of the Ashmead report. "Should you care to know more [about Bergel's] strengths and weaknesses," she added, "I shall be very glad to talk to you about them." The headmaster never replied. The Ashmead report said it all. Bergel did not get the job.[31]

Bergel remained unemployed for almost three years. It was not until late in 1937, Mrs. Bergel recalls, that "my friends in Cranford labored to get Lienhard a job in the high school. Hardly had he started there, when he was called to Queens College."[32]

That proved to be the big break of Bergel's career. Queens College, a public institution in New York City, had opened its doors in 1937. It desperately needed teachers in all fields, and the head of the German Department knew Bergel and admired his skills. He hired him as an instructor in 1938. Shortly thereafter, Bergel entered the graduate program at New York University to obtain an American Ph.D. He could hardly believe his good fortune. At the age of thirty-three, his academic career was back on track once again.*

---

* In his various articles on the Bergel-Hauptmann case, *Home News* reporter Peter Parisi wrote that Dr. Bergel "went on to a distinguished career in comparative literature" and retired "after helping to establish the graduate school of the City University of New York." (See, for example, New Brunswick *Home News*, May 5, 16, 1985.) Bergel did not publish his first article until 1947, more than a decade after he left N.J.C. He published perhaps a dozen articles in his forty-year career. Our committee could find no evidence that Dr. Bergel helped to establish the graduate school at CUNY, although he did teach there as an adjunct professor in

In New Brunswick, meanwhile, Hauptmann appeared shaken—almost unhappy—in victory. The press had ridiculed him; politicians had lambasted him; colleagues and students had testified against him. Even worse, the hearings had aggravated his most pressing problem: his enormous personal debt. At the beginning of 1935, he already owed creditors almost five thousand dollars, a sum greater than the Hauptmanns' combined yearly income. He had large medical bills. His family made regular trips to Germany. He owed money to banks, bookstores, department stores, doctors, and dozens of local merchants.

Financially, the hearings almost crushed him. He had planned to present his own case to the trustees. But then Bergel got himself a lawyer, free of charge, and Hauptmann changed his mind. He hired Fred G. Tauber, an experienced attorney, who charged $1,500 for his services. Hauptmann believed, mistakenly, that Rutgers would pay part of his fee. "I had hoped for some financial help in carrying a burden that equals almost half a year's salary," he complained to President Clothier. "However, it seems that my hope is not to be realized."[33]

Clothier had little sympathy for Hauptmann's plight. Indeed, he apparently tried to "dump" Hauptmann after the hearings by offering to "exchange" him for a professor from a small college in Tennessee. "He was ready to get rid of [him]," Dean Meder recalled. "And Ashmead heard about it and vetoed. He said 'You can't do that. That would impugn the findings of your own committee.'"[34]

Early in 1936 Corwin and Clothier agreed to meet with Hauptmann about his "problem." Their aim was to protect Rutgers from further embarrassment, and this meant keeping its most controversial figure from declaring bankruptcy. According to Corwin's notes

---

the 1970s. Peter Parisi admitted to our committee that he never bothered to get a copy of Bergel's vitae. When asked how he knew that Bergel had enjoyed a "distinguished" career in comparative literature, Parisi replied that Bergel had told him so. For Bergel's vitae, see Bergel Family Correspondence File, Rutgers University Archives.

of the meeting, four issues were discussed. First, Mrs. Hauptmann's dismissal would not be reconsidered; that would be a public relations disaster. Second, Hauptmann's salary would be raised *after* the University took care of "other departments worse off than his." Third, while Rutgers could not lend Hauptmann the money to pay off his debts, it would try to assist him in other ways. Fourth, Hauptmann had to clear up his citizenship problem as quickly as possible. As Corwin noted, "He [must] decide in which country he wants to live and act accordingly—not try to straddle."[35]

A short time later President Clothier "assisted" Hauptmann by introducing him to Richard Segoine, head of the Rutgers Alumni Council. Hauptmann had never met Segoine, but he did know his daughter. During the hearings, Bergel claimed to have raised the grade of a student, Elizabeth Segoine, after receiving a "sudden telephone call" from Hauptmann. "You can't give her a D," Hauptmann said. "The administration is very much concerned because her father has some business with the University and he cannot be annoyed." Hauptmann did not deny the story.[36]

In any event, Segoine was anxious to help. He promised Hauptmann that he would contact a man who knew Rutgers "from every angle," and he proved true to his word. On August 21, 1936, Segoine wrote to J. Edward Ashmead about Hauptmann's "predicament." "I believe he is sincere in wishing to pay his creditors in full," said Segoine. "I took the liberty of referring him to you because . . . you are one of the few persons whose advice in this particular area might be helpful."[37]

Hauptmann met privately with Ashmead the following month. He was looking for a large loan, and he appeared optimistic about getting one. But his hopes were dashed temporarily when Ashmead died of cancer that fall. (The university's tribute, written by Segoine, was titled "Above All Else—A Rutgers Man.")[38]

By this point, however, saving Hauptmann from bankruptcy had become a high priority to Clothier and Corwin. They approached another trustee, John Wycoff Mettler, the wealthy industrialist who had sat with Ashmead on the investigating committee. Mettler endorsed a large note for Hauptmann, and the crisis appeared to be over.

Dean Corwin was obviously relieved. She wrote a letter to Mettler thanking him for his generosity. Mettler's reply proved to be prophetic, indeed. "I realize that I may be 'sticking out my neck,'" he said. "I remember Baron Rothschild's famous remark: 'Never have anything to do with an unlucky man or an unlucky place—there is usually a reason."[39]

In retrospect, the university's handling of this matter was disturbing, to say the least. For one thing, Rutgers had done for Hauptmann, secretly, what it refused to do for others. (Faculty members who incurred embarrasing debts were routinely induced to resign.) For another, the rescue process had involved the most powerful and self-interested members of the Rutgers family: Clothier, Corwin, Ashmead, Mettler, and Segoine. John Mettler well understood this, though he jokingly explained the intervention in benevolent terms. "Anyway, it is Christmas-time," he told Dean Corwin, "and, of course, there are a lot of Santa Clauses these days."[40]

8 THE COVER-UP

By 1937 the University seemed to be recovering a bit from the effects of the Great Depression. The New Jersey Legislature had just restored some of the devastating budget cuts of 1932 and 1933: salaries could be cautiously increased and new faculty hired. One of the first beneficiaries of this modest upswing was the ubiquitous Professor Hauptmann at N.J.C. On July 1 Dean Corwin informed him that his salary would be raised by $300 a year, thereby keeping a promise she had made some time before. Apparently, however, Corwin's generosity caught one Rutgers official by surprise. "In my judgment it is a mistake to increase Hauptmann," wrote comptroller A. S. Johnson to President Clothier. "I feel we are playing with fire. Since [Hauptmann] has already been told by Miss Corwin . . . it is now too late to do anything about it. I really feel this is most unfortunate."[1]

In September 1937 German course enrollments at N.J.C. went up for the first time in years. Quite naturally, Hauptmann appealed to Corwin for help. With the dismissal of Bergel in 1935, and of Mrs. Hauptmann in 1937, the German Department was down to three people—Emil Jordan, Alice Schlimbach, and Hauptmann himself. After studying the budget and enrollment figures, Corwin allowed the department to hire a new instructor at $1,800 a year.

The leading candidate was Werner Hollmann, a young scholar from Germany. The son of a Lutheran minister, Hollmann had come to America in 1934 after receiving a doctorate in journalism from the University of Munich. As usual, Dean Corwin took part in the hiring process. In Hollmann's case, however, her interest was certainly sharpened by the recent troubles at N.J.C. Writing directly to President Ada Comstock of Radcliffe College, one of Hollmann's references, Corwin said: "We . . . prefer . . . a man who [is] interested first in language, literature, and culture, rather than in politics. Do you feel that Mr. Hollman would be a strong devotee of one type of government as opposed to another?"[2]

Comstock's reply was reassuring. Hollmann "seems . . . an exceptionally fine young man," she wrote. "He is not, I believe, an adherent of the present regime [in Germany]; but he has found it possible to live under it, and in the conversations I have had with him he has seemed . . . to be much more interested in intellectual and cultural questions than in politics."[3]

Hollmann was hired by N.J.C. in October 1937. He worked as an instructor until 1940, when he was promoted to the rank of assistant professor. He left the College in 1946 to join the faculty of Princeton University.[4]

On March 8, 1939, Hauptmann became a naturalized citizen of the United States. He was accompanied by Albert Meder and Albert Holzmann, who acted as witnesses. Hauptmann viewed this process as a necessity, not an honor. He knew that his job at Rutgers depended on it. Significantly, Mrs. Hauptmann did not become a citizen; she saw no reason to follow her husband's lead.[5]

These were difficult times for the Hauptmanns. Their feelings for the "Fatherland" were very strong. Hauptmann himself had wanted to return to Germany permanently in 1937. He stayed on, he recalled, because the "Reich representative" had urged him to "serve the cultural-political interests of the Reich" in New Jersey. Nevertheless, the Hauptmanns had sent their American-born daughters Gudrun and Sieglinde to attend school in Germany under the supervision of a young housekeeper. This move had surprised Hauptmann's colleagues because the family was perpetually in debt and because events in Europe seemed to be leading to war. According to immigration records, Mrs. Hauptmann spent four months with her daughters in the Marburg area in 1938. When the Nazis attacked Poland the following year, the Hauptmanns were frantic. Hauptmann approached the State Department for assistance. He was told that his children would be "evacuated to neutral

Denmark in the event their safety was in any way compromised."
This was hardly reassuring news. The girls returned to New Brunswick a few months later.[6]

Although Hauptmann had not made any public statements
about the Nazis during this period, his admiration for Hitler was
apparent to the people he trusted. When Emil Jordan returned from
a trip to Germany in 1939, Hauptmann pumped him for information. "[His] first question," Jordan remembered, "was 'Did you go
to Nuremberg [and] take part in the festivities there?'" When Jordan replied that he had "kept away from the Nazis," Hauptmann
was furious. He could not understand how a German could "miss
the opportunity to visit the Nazi shrines, to meet at least some of
the new great leaders."[7]

Jordan recalled that "another development came to a head" in
1939, and it was sadly familiar. "Right from the beginning," he
said, "Hauptmann had borrowed money from me, 200, 300, 400 or
more dollars. When he repaid a loan, he came for another one a
short time later. That I decided to stop. . . . There was quite a confrontation. He seemed to consider me a traitor to Germany and
to Hauptmann himself, and from that moment on . . . he did not
talk to me."[8]

Hauptmann was again in debt, begging money from banks and
colleagues and friends. He borrowed hundreds of dollars from Albert Meder, the Jamesburg National Bank, and even the father of
one of his students. In March 1940 he made a desperate attempt to
reverse his financial position. He purchased a beauty parlor in
Newark, New Jersey, for $1,500, half down and half by year's end.
Marie Hauptmann managed the shop, known as Albert's Hairdresser, on a full-time basis. But the business did poorly, and the
Hauptmanns seemed worse off than before.[9]

On October 1, 1940, Dean Corwin summoned Hauptmann to
her office. She did so at the "request" of President Clothier, who
feared that members of the German Department might embarrass
the University by making pro-Nazi statements in public. Europe
was now in shambles. Hitler had annexed Austria, carved up
Czechoslovakia, and signed a non-aggression pact with the Russians. His armies had invaded and conquered Denmark, Norway,

Belgium, the Netherlands, France, and most of Poland. Only England stood in Hitler's path, and her future looked bleak. President Franklin D. Roosevelt, campaigning for a third term in 1940, was determined to keep Britain afloat. The American people were overwhelmingly sympathetic to England, but anxious to stay out of war.

Corwin's notes of this fateful meeting are worth quoting:

> Hauptmann said he would be most careful about trying to keep content of class work to non-political matters. . . . [While] he is an American citizen . . . he cannot change his position re the German government. While he would never do anything against the U.S.A., he could not fall in line with the present American attitude (that is, in his opinion, if you are not pro-British you are anti-American). He pointed out that Mrs. Hauptmann is still a German citizen and will not change to American citizenship. He will be just as careful as he knows how to avoid any possible complication or embarrassment for the University.[10]

Hauptmann offered a different version of this meeting. He claimed that Corwin had stressed the duties of citizenship, the importance of protecting the University, and the need to *accept* "the 'English-American' point of view." When Hauptmann replied that he could never renounce his homeland, Corwin asked him "what then would be [his] future plans." Hauptmann was stunned. The dean was pressing him to resign. Her intent was "unmistakable."[11]

Hauptmann told his wife about the meeting. Some years later he recalled that she "decided against my wishes and advice to leave for Germany with my two daughters." Her reasons were simple. She feared her husband "might have again to face difficulties [like the Bergel incident] and . . . she thought she would improve the [financial] situation of the family by going." Hauptmann added: "I am very much attached to my family, there was no other way out, I had to follow them."[12]

On November 10 Hauptmann informed the dean that he would be "unable to attend classes for some time as the condition of my kidneys is so bad that I have to stay in bed." Two days later in an emotional letter to President Clothier he spelled out the "main reason" for his absence. "The insoluble question," he said, "is: Shall I be loyal to the land of my forefathers to which I owe absolutely everything . . . or shall I be loyal to the University which I have had the honor to teach in now for thirteen long and fruitful years?"

The answer came as no surprise. "Since I cannot adapt myself to the political stand which the University seems to require . . . ," Hauptmann continued, "it appears to me best that I should drop out as quietly as possible. The possibility is afforded by my state of health. . . . My kidneys are badly infected. . . . During this time of recovering Mrs. Hauptmann will have to take care of my family and myself: and the task will be very difficult."

Hauptmann did want something in return, however: a year's leave of absence on full salary. The money would be deposited in his bank account for the payment of debts. "Unless this request is granted," he went on, "it will be necessary for me to declare my bankruptcy. I am anxious to avoid this both for myself and for the University." Hauptmann concluded: "I shall not require a reply to this letter since I am unable at the present time to give any definite address as I do not know where I am going to establish my residence. The statements from my bank will be sufficient evidence that my request for a leave of absence has been granted."[13]

Clothier sent the letter to Dean Corwin, for he wanted her advice. Corwin replied that a "definite agreement" with Hauptmann was now essential. Hauptmann's letter was ambiguous; he certainly implied that he was leaving, but he had not *officially* resigned. The next step, therefore, was to locate Hauptmann and nail down the particulars. "If he resigns in a business-like way . . . ," said Corwin, "I feel that we should carry his full salary until June 30, 1941. If not, [we should] withhold further payments on his salary since he himself cut us off from communicating with him."[14]

For the next several days, Corwin and Clothier were in constant contact about the Hauptmann response. On this issue, at least, the dean was clearly in command. Clothier did not make a move without consulting her; and she did not leave much to chance. On November 20, still unable to locate Hauptmann, she warned the president: "You will, I know, want to move just as cautiously and thoughtfully and wisely as we can in this matter to avoid another *cause célèbre*. The fact that the central figure now is the very one whom we defended in the Bergel case leaves us in a very exposed position. If our present action indicates that the Civil Liberties Union was right in 1936, they will not hesitate to bring it out in the headlines." [15]

On November 23 Corwin reiterated the need for "caution" and "coordination." "If we have to share our correspondence with an investigating committee of any sort," she wrote, "we want to have it as wise and considered as possible. . . . I cannot say how strongly I feel that we must do everything to avoid panic and implied suspicion since not only our own procedure with subsequent civil rights and academic investigating agencies is involved but also in all probability a government investigating agency." [16]

Corwin knew that Hauptmann was gone, perhaps for good. His salary payments were stopped on November 19, the day after an N.J.C. staffer visited his home. The staffer reported: "Found papers for two weeks stacked up there. Landlady said Hauptmann had paid his rent—moved out suddenly 1 a.m." The University sent a registered letter to his beauty parlor in Newark; it was returned "unclaimed." A check with the New Brunswick Post Office showed that Hauptmann had left a forwarding address—General Delivery, Miami, Florida. But no one picked up the mail that was sent there. [17]

There were immediate rumors that Hauptmann had left for Germany. Clothier and Corwin learned the facts in January 1941. They were informed by a member of the Rutgers German Department, most likely Albert Holzmann, who had heard of Hauptmann's whereabouts while attending a language convention in New York City. Someone at N.J.C., probably Corwin herself, then phoned the FBI. On January 22 the agent in charge of the case reported that "MARIE HAUPTMANN and her two children had sailed from New York to Lisbon; that Germany is their ultimate destination; that JOHANNES HAUPTMANN had left for California where he was going to sail for Japan with Germany as his ultimate destination." [18]

In the following weeks Corwin's office was flooded with inquiries from Hauptmann's creditors. The list was impressive: Bamberger's, Strechert Bookstore, Style Dress Shop, Davega Radio

Store, Charles Weber Coal Company, and Sears, Roebuck, to name a few. Corwin received an angry note from the man who had sold Hauptmann the beauty parlor (and still had $750 coming to him). He wanted to know whether Hauptmann had left behind any assets or uncashed checks. (He had not.) The Jamesburg National Bank sent a letter, as did the Morris Plan Bank of New York, which had loaned Hauptmann $728 on October 31, 1940. That money had obviously been used to finance the family's trip back to Germany.[19]

Corwin and Clothier did not volunteer information about Hauptmann's departure. They told the FBI and perhaps a few officials of the University what they knew. They did not tell the press, the creditors, or even the police chief of New Brunswick, who assumed the Hauptmanns had fled to Mexico. Corwin's statement to reporters was misleading. She said: "Professor Hauptmann asked for a leave of absence because of ill health. This was arranged. . . . [He] has not taught here since September 9. He did not leave a forwarding address or give us any information whatsoever as to where he was going." Corwin did not mention Hauptmann's "conflicting loyalties" or his apparent intention to leave the college for good. She did not say that his paychecks had been stopped or that he had almost certainly departed for Germany.

Corwin's personal letters on the subject were even worse. On January 30, 1941, she told a creditor: "I realize fully that it must sound rather odd, but we have absolutely no knowledge of the whereabouts of Professor Hauptmann and his family." This was not true. The FBI report on Hauptmann's disappearance had been filed the week before. The FBI agent had interviewed a number of people at Rutgers and N.J.C. Although the names are blacked out, it is not hard to determine that these people included Corwin, Holzmann, and Meder—all of whom had some "knowledge" of Hauptmann's "whereabouts."[20]

On March 10 Corwin told reporters that she had still not heard from the missing professor. She did not mention his likely flight to Germany. Corwin did say—rather remarkably—that his disappearance was "entirely inexplicable." And she "intimated" that Hauptmann would be formally dismissed by the Board of Trustees in the near future.

On May 2 President Clothier sent Hauptmann a one-sentence letter. "This is to inform you," it said, "that by the authority of the Trustees of the University your appointment as Associate Professor of German will be terminated as of June 30, 1941." Hauptmann did not receive the letter; it was mailed to his old New Brunswick address. But Corwin and Clothier assumed that the case had now been closed, with virtually no damage done to the University. And that was the best news of all.[21]

Hauptmann's years in Germany will be described in the next chapter. Before following him there, however, we need to consider one final question: Was Hauptmann involved in espionage or other questionable activities for the Nazi government during his time in the United States?

Hauptmann's FBI file is filled with allegations by unnamed informants. They include the following: that Hauptmann "received considerable mail from foreign places"; that he had "a good many pictures of Fort Hancock," which he may or may not have placed in the lining of a trunk; that he "made suspicious contacts" with the German vessels *Bremen* and *Europa* when they docked in New York Harbor; and that he "and an unidentified woman doctor" rented a cottage at Sandy Hook in the summer of 1934 "and there spent many hours observing and studying the details of [Army] maneuvers."[22]

These allegations are flimsy, to say the least. Hauptmann may have received many letters from Germany, but an FBI "mail cover" did not turn up anything suspicious. The informant who spoke about Hauptmann's trunk admitted that his theory "was merely hearsay on his part." It is true that Hauptmann visited German vessels when they docked in New York harbor, but so did hundreds of other people. And one informant, who described Hauptmann as "definitely pro-German," said the professor went aboard "for the purpose of having a conversation and refreshing his memories of Germany." There is nothing in Hauptmann's file to refute or substantiate this perception.[23]

The charge that Hauptmann and a female doctor observed "Army maneuvers" at Sandy Hook in 1934 is also unconvincing.

Emil Jordan recalled that the Hauptmanns were friendly with a woman who owned a home overlooking the ocean in Atlantic Highlands. The woman was a doctor who frequently invited the Hauptmanns and the Jordans for visits in the summer months. Furthermore, the "maneuvers" they supposedly "studied" were not maneuvers at all. As the Secretary of War reported: "In September of 1934, a . . . command post exercise was held in New Jersey. . . . Unfortunately money was not available for the concentration of troops so only commanders and staffs participated." This was hardly surprising. The full strength of the American army in 1934 was only 118,000.[24]

The most serious allegations against Hauptmann were leveled by Bergel. In a long interview with the FBI in 1943, Bergel claimed that Hauptmann had been told by the German Consul General in New York "to establish a Nazi cell at [N.J.C.] with himself as head . . . to disseminate propaganda favorable to Nazi ideology." Bergel went on to say that Emil Jordan and Alice Schlimbach were "very much enthused about these efforts" and "would frequently meet with Hauptmann for the sole purpose of planning the advancement of the Nazi cause." According to Bergel, at least, "The latter two individuals were so closely associated with Hauptmann . . . that their position [toward Nazi Germany] was less dangerous to the United States only because they were subordinates of Hauptmann and not themselves actually leaders of a Nazi cell."[25]

It is worth noting that Bergel did not make any of these bold and damning statements during his lengthy testimony before the Ashmead committee in 1935—at a time when they would have been well publicized and severely challenged. It is also significant that the voluminous files of the FBI provide no evidence to substantiate Bergel's allegations. There is simply nothing in Hauptmann's file, or Bergel's file, or the so-called German archives file, to back up his remarkable interview in 1943.

Nevertheless, one entry in Hauptmann's FBI file is certainly intriguing. It is a short, cryptic telegram from the German Foreign Office to the German Consulate in New York. And it reads: "In consideration of the peculiar circumstances of the case as described in your report of November 11, 1940—Kult b XX—will agree, as an exception, that the costs involving the repatriation of Professor Johann Hauptmann may be finally charged by analogous use of Section Four of the Circular Order of June 26, 1940." Put simply, the Nazi government had paid for Hauptmann's trip back to Germany.[26]

Why was this done? What were the "peculiar circumstances" surrounding Hauptmann's case? We know that the German Consul General and the German Foreign Office were very interested in the Bergel-Hauptmann hearings. We also know that several German-American organizations and German language newspapers viewed Hauptmann as both a victim of anti-Nazi elements and a symbol of German pride in America. It seems likely, therefore, that Hauptmann's claim upon the Berlin government rested largely on his reputation as a martyr, a man who had suffered dearly for his support of the "Fatherland." As we shall see, this perception of Hauptmann—which the professor carefully nurtured and embellished—would continue to pay big dividends in Germany during World War II.[27]

9 WORKING FOR THE NAZIS

The reasons for Hauptmann's disappearance from New Brunswick in November 1940 have long remained obscure. We know now that the German Foreign Office appreciated his "sacrifices" for the Fatherland at Rutgers University. When Hauptmann expressed a desire to return to Germany in 1937, he was persuaded by German consular officials to continue serving "the cultural-political interests of the Reich" in New Jersey. Two years later, Hauptmann acquired American citizenship after consulting with the Consulate in New York. This led to the loss of his German citizenship, which created grave problems when he was confronted by Dean Corwin's ultimatum that he either adopt an Anglo-American line or face the possibility of losing his job. Turning once more to the Consulate, he was told that the time had come for him to leave the country.

Hauptmann's wife and two daughters encountered no problems in returning to the Fatherland by ship via Bilboa, Spain, because they held German passports. For Hauptmann, matters were not so simple. Now an American citizen, he discovered that he could not get a passport. In his quandary, he spoke with consular officials, who instructed him to file for the restoration of his German citizenship; then he was issued an alien passport (*Fremdenpass*) that enabled him to make an easy departure from San Francisco to Yokohama, Japan. After obtaining a transit visa (*Reisepass*) from the local consul there, Hauptmann returned to Germany by way of Korea, Manchuria, the Trans-Siberian Railroad to Moscow, and a final train to Berlin.[1]

Soon after his arrival, Hauptmann went to the Foreign Office to find employment. When his American citizenship created some difficulties, he called at both the Cultural-Political Department of the Foreign Office and the Foreign Organization of the Nazi Party. His problem disappeared when he persuaded a government official to obtain telegraphic confirmation of his story from the New York consulate.[2]

On February 20, 1941, Hauptmann applied for membership in the Nazi Party, possibly to enhance his job prospects. His membership, dated April 1, had the party number 8,843,729. With his credentials now in order, he was given a job at the Goethe Institute of the *Deutsche Akademie* (German Academy). At first he had a temporary assignment translating and revising a technical reader. As the book neared completion, a better position materialized. The Foreign Office felt indebted to Hauptmann, and, "on its own volition," suggested that he become the Academy's national leader or *Mittelstellenleiter* for Slovakia. The Party's Foreign Office also came to his aid. Declaring that he had a "moral claim" for having served the interests of the Reich in America, it recommended that Hauptmann be given an "exceptional subvention" to furnish his new living quarters.[3]

With his appointment as *Mittelstellenleiter* of the German Academy in Slovakia, Hauptmann could take pride in a prestigious position. He could also maintain his family in comfort and indulge his propensity for acting the role of fussy bureaucrat. The Academy's headquarters were in Bratislava, which the Germans called Pressburg. The city was the capital of Slovakia, a puppet state created by Germany out of a remnant of Czechoslovakia in 1939.[4]

The Academy had been founded in Munich in 1925 by a group of German nationalists who helped shape the Nazi concept of *Lebensraum* (living space). Its main objective was to expand Germany's influence throughout the world by spreading the use of the German language and exalting the richness of German culture. The Academy was a small operation before the Nazis came to power; it conducted only six schools of *lektorate*, mainly in southeastern Europe. After 1933, when Rudolf Hess, the Deputy Fuehrer, took the Academy under his patronage, it became increasingly identified with the National Socialist Party. By 1937 the number of schools had swelled to forty-four. The transition to full Nazi management was completed in November 1941, when Hitler signed a decree that ended the Academy's private status and transformed it into a public corporation.[5]

Like many Nazi agencies, the Academy was placed under multiple, and not entirely harmonious, jurisdictions. Responsibility for its overall direction was vested in the Propaganda Ministry, headed by Joseph Goebbels, but its operations outside Germany were controlled by the Foreign Ministry. With regard to the Bratislava branch, Hauptmann's superior was the German Ambassador to Slovakia, who usually acted through his Cultural Attache.[6]

Hauptmann's position was no sinecure; his two predecessors had been fired for ideological and administrative shortcomings. He had to remain in the good graces of his superiors, especially the Cultural Attache. He had to deal with his staff of *lectors* throughout Slovakia, who were sometimes reluctant to acknowledge his authority. And he had to cope with the tricky problem of confused jurisdiction. The policies of the Propaganda Ministry, the Foreign Office, the Foreign Office of the Nazi Party, the Ethnic German Central Office, the S.S. and S.D. toward Slovakia were perpetually in conflict. Not surprisingly, Hauptmann was often bewildered by the morass that was the Nazi bureaucracy and uncertain how to conduct himself.[7]

Of one thing Hauptmann was sure: he wanted to live well. His extravagant behavior in Slovakia was a virtual replay of his days in New Brunswick. He complained about his salary, placed his wife on the Academy payroll, borrowed heavily to furnish an apartment, and demanded a grand piano and a car. His logic was interesting: a respectable life style was necessary to uphold German prestige in Slovakia. He even claimed that his Italian counterparts lived better than he did.[8]

Hauptmann's duties as "national leader" of the Academy in Slovakia were manifold. Of chief importance were his administrative responsibilities. He supervised a large staff, a library, and a cultural institute; he arranged for the distribution of films and records, and busied himself with a limitless flow of paperwork. More satisfying, no doubt, were the occasions when he represented the Academy at "cultural events" in Bratislava and other towns; there he could stand forth as an important figure.

Hauptmann complained that these burdens left little time for teaching. His predecessors had taught sixteen hours a week. Hauptmann began with a six-hour schedule, teaching German language and literature. He soon cut this to four hours, despite repeated warnings from his superiors in Munich. Mrs. Hauptmann, in contrast, taught twenty hours a week.[9]

Hauptmann's role was to disseminate a correct version of German culture, along with outright propaganda. Here, too, he was dilatory. He gave a number of lectures in various towns and cities, but all of them dealt with conditions in the United States, a topic of remote relevance to the Slovaks. He did not affiliate with any of the numerous organizations such as the *Deutsche Partei* of ethnic Germans in Slovakia, which advocated a radical policy of Germanization within the puppet state. In such matters, he maintained a policy of cautious reserve. This attitude was manifest in his training of German ethnic teachers, in his reluctance to allow the *lectors* to act as informants for the German Embassy, and above all in his avoidance of any connection with the notorious S.S. or the S.D.[10]

His record at Bratislava was not that of a "rabid" Nazi, but he followed the orders of his superiors, accepted their racial ideology, and adhered to the Nazi line on the "Jewish Question." When he visited the Herman Goering Works in Waag-Bystric, for example, and discovered that German courses were being taught there by an ethnic whose wife was Jewish, he viewed the man's retention with "the most serious reservations." A bit later, he recommended that the building in which the Academy rented its quarters be purchased from the Slovak State, despite the fact that it had been confiscated because the previous owner was a Jew. In his most ideologically charged statement, Hauptmann deplored the fact that "Jewish literature still makes its way into the country" and that "the work of Emil Ludwig and other immigrants" was available at the local bookstores.

There was more. Hauptmann's callousness was on full display when he complained, in 1944, about "the large number of Jews . . . still present in Slovakia." By this time, he almost certainly knew the fate of the Slovak Jews who were being deported to death camps in the east. In another context, he suggested that the Slovaks were not receptive to German influence because their "Slavic blood" made them amenable to Russian propaganda. "After all," he explained, "blood is drawn to blood." [11]

Hauptmann in Bratislava is best understood as a man determined to advance his career, increase his fortune, and acquire the status and respect he craved. He was repeatedly disappointed that his past sufferings for the Reich and his new appointment as *Mittelstellenleiter* did not earn him the recognition he desired. In 1942, for example, he became extremely embittered when a personal conflict with the Cultural Attache caused him to lose the positions he coveted the most, the executive management of the German Cultural Institute in Bratislava and the leadership of a German Information Library. Although he complained that he had suffered "the greatest trial" ever endured by a German in America, he could not prevail over the ambitions of his direct superior. [12]

Furthermore, when his authority was challenged by his fractious *lectors*, Hauptmann showed the same sensitivity he had displayed at N.J.C. He expected absolute deference and resented those who outshone him or questioned his leadership. In one instance, he described a subordinate's behavior this way: "Since Golombek . . . is evidently intent on letting the leader of the *Mittelstelle* know that he regards him as a complete non-entity . . . I am hereby compelled to announce that I am not willing to sit by idly while I am being circumvented." A more serious clash occurred in 1943. The *lector*, a German-Czech named Julius Mader, was younger than Hauptmann, better educated, and extremely ambitious. Mader had ingratiated himself with the German S.S. in Slovakia by sounding and acting like a model Nazi. He insisted, however, that his superior credentials, his high standing with the local leadership, and his popularity as a *lector* had all served to turn Hauptmann against him. According to Mader, his work at Bratislava received "universal praise" from everyone but "the leader of the [*Mittelstelle*], who not once . . . displayed any interest in it. . . . On the contrary, I had the distinct feeling that my successful work, which he could hardly begin to match, irked him a great deal (*sehr wider den Strich ging*)."

Before long, Mader added, he was assigned to a variety of menial jobs. Hauptmann and his wife treated him like a servant; at one point, they ordered him to move heavy furniture about their apartment. When Mader resisted, Hauptmann called him "dirt lazy" and threatened to send him to the Eastern Front. Mader complained directly to the Academy's headquarters in Munich, but the authorities were not very receptive. Their main objectives, it seemed, were to maintain order within the organization and to preserve the chain of command. As a result, Hauptmann escaped punishment, despite his admission that he had used vulgar language in dealing with a subordinate. Poor Mader did not fare as well. For registering his complaint (and thus insulting his superior), he received a severe reprimand and a transfer to an obscure post in Debrezcen, Hungary.[13]

As advancing Russian armies approached Slovakia late in 1944, a disheartened Hauptmann looked to the future with apprehension. There are indications that he may have been under a small cloud in Bratislava. In November 1944 Professor Matthias Schmitz, the Academy's Secretary General, made a cryptic reference to Hauptmann's "negotiating directly with other Ministries." Apparently the infraction was not serious. The Academy still worked diligently for Hauptmann, attempting to obtain for him both a War Service Medal and a position in post-war Germany at the rank of *Oberregierungsrat*, or Senior Government Councillor. There were further charges that he did not report some currency transactions to the satisfaction of the Germany Academy. But nothing came of them either.[14]

In any event, one could scarcely conclude that Hauptmann was a die-hard Nazi, ready to make any sacrifice for the crumbling Third Reich. In fact, during the last days of the war, he showed himself to be the very opposite. He abandoned his post in Bratislava without permission and fled to Altenmarkt, Austria, in mid-February 1945. Refusing to render an account to his superiors, who were quartered in a castle called Schloss Hoech, above the town, Hauptmann insisted that he needed to find housing for his wife. He bluntly declared: "I shall do what I want!" His startled superior responded: "It simply will not do . . . that a *Mittelstellenleiter* . . .

should continually set himself above all regulations and demand a special status for himself." [15]

Despite Hauptmann's insubordination, his superiors kept in touch with him and requested his cooperation. But he was not amenable. By now he had broken off direct contact with the officials at the castle and was living in Altenmarkt with his wife, his two daughters, and his former secretary, Frauelein Schisma. In June of 1945, however, he suddenly appeared at the Academy's headquarters in Munich. After reporting that the castle had still not been taken by American troops, Hauptmann revealed the real reasons for his trip. First, he wanted to resume work for the Academy by starting up courses in English, the language of the victors. Second, he hoped to learn the status of his American citizenship. Having it, he thought, would smooth his dealings with the occupation forces. Finally—as always—he demanded money, claiming that he had not been paid since March. When he heard that the Academy's accounts were closed and that the Academy itself might be abolished soon he demanded severance pay. Four months later, he was still badgering the Academy for help to return to Germany so that he could join his family. [16]

The story of Hauptmann's arrest has many versions. Edward Cap, a former instructor at Rutgers College, wrote excitedly to Professor Holzmann on March 11, 1946, that he had helped to capture "one of Dr. Goebbels' agents. . . . Yes, it was the N.J.C. Hauptmann!" Cap, an American Intelligence Officer, had recognized a photo of Hauptmann among some captured enemy documents, ascertained that he was living in Altenmarkt, and informed the FBI. Hauptmann was then picked up and interned in October 1945. Three months later, the *New Brunswick Sunday Times* featured a sensational report by former Major Edwin A. Baldwin, who claimed that *he* had been responsible for Hauptmann's arrest in August 1945, well before Cap had alerted the FBI. As Baldwin described it, Hauptmann was then living with his wife in a "lonely castle, known as Schloss Hoech . . . whose main tower dates back to 1,000 A.D." The castle, he said, contained all sorts of files about Nazi agents throughout the world. (The files were doubtless those of the *Deutsche*

Akademie.) Baldwin remembered apprehending three professors, Hauptmann included, as they fled in an old car filled with propaganda material and records.[17]

Precisely where the Hauptmanns were living in August 1945 and the circumstances of his arrest remain unclear. Irene Helms Hardcastle, who devoted many years to an extraordinarily detailed study of the German Academy, claims that the three men arrested near Schloss Hoech were Dr. Stroedel, Richard Wold, and *Lector* Daniel Wenzel. Hauptmann is never mentioned in her microscopic history.[18]

For his part, Hauptmann told an Army interrogator that he had reported himself to the office of military government in Radstatt in July 1945. On December 27 he was picked up by the Counter Intelligence Corps, imprisoned in St. Johann, Austria, and transferred to Camp Marcus W. Orr. There he remained in custody until November 1946, when he was freed under local arrest and sent back to Altenmarkt. The following year Hauptmann was repatriated to Germany after being deemed a German citizen. When he returned to Austria illegally, he was again apprehended in September 1947, interrogated, and released.[19]

The revelation that Hauptmann had served the German cause did not seem to bother the authorities in Washington. In June 1947, however, Bergel wrote to the War Crimes Branch to inquire why nothing was being done. He enclosed newspaper clippings that alleged that Hauptmann had committed treason. Bergel's letter was referred to the Department of Justice. After reviewing its files on Hauptmann, the agency concluded that the information was insufficient to warrant further investigation, but it did request the Civil Affairs Division of the Army to probe more deeply into Hauptmann's wartime employment. It added that the State Department might be interested in the event that Hauptmann sought a passport to return to the United States.[20]

It was in response to this suggestion that the Army War Crimes Group arrested Hauptmann in September 1947, lodged him in the city jail of Salzburg, and questioned him. Unfortunately, the interrogation process was very poor. No one there knew enough to challenge Hauptmann's preposterous assertions that he had lectured at the Academy on the writings of Heinrich Heine, a great German-Jewish author, or that he had purposely chosen an Eastern assignment (Slovakia) so as not to harm "English-American interests" during the war. While the full text of this interrogation was sent to the Department of Justice, it did not result in any proceedings against Hauptmann. As far as can be ascertained, he was never prosecuted for any offenses, despite his numerous arrests.[21]

For unknown reasons, Hauptmann chose to spend the rest of his life in Austria, rather than in Germany. Back in Altenmarkt, he registered as a German citizen, then switched to American citizenship, and finally listed himself as "stateless." Having no known employment or visible means of support, he sought to establish a new life for himself.[22]

In 1949 his wife Marie went back to America to join their daughters, who were living on Long Island. Hauptmann tried to return as well. Invoking the aid of a former U.S. Director for Refugee Affairs, he vainly sought permission to enter the United States. Perhaps in response to the Justice Department's recommendation, the State Department revoked his American citizenship on August 20, 1949. Although Mrs. Hauptmann made periodic visits to Austria until 1968, there are indications that their marriage foundered and ended in divorce.[23]

When Hauptmann moved to Salzburg in 1951, he was sixty-one years old. He lived for years without any known means of support. He did find marginal employment between 1959 and 1964; during that time he worked for a few months a year at the international summer courses for the German Language and German Studies in Salzburg and at neighboring Castle Klessheim. According to the published brochure of that program, conducted for foreign students, he never gave any public lectures; his teaching evidently was confined to basic German language courses. Hauptmann must have received a meager salary since he performed a job ordinarily held by student assistants or new teachers to supplement their regular pay.[24]

Hauptmann died on December 29, 1978, at the age of eighty-eight. His death stirred no attention; it was merely mentioned by the local papers under the general column "deceased." There were no other death notices or obituaries. So obscure was Hauptmann that he was buried in a communal tomb that served as a last resting place for a number of families. The only reminder of his tempestuous existence was a separate stone bearing his name.[25]

EPILOGUE

On December 17, 1986, our committee released an Interim Report on the Bergel-Hauptmann case at a press conference in the Rutgers Library. To our amazement, the spacious New Jersey Room was standing room only; reporters, photographers, and spectators filled every seat and lined the back wall. There were representatives from the wire services, the *New York Times*, *Newsday*, the *Newark Star Ledger*, the *Trenton Evening Times*, the *Hackensack Record*, the *New Brunswick Home News*, and a dozen other papers. The following day brought a flurry of attention. There were stories about our findings, interviews with Bergel, and denunciations by Alan Silver, who held an informal press conference of his own. Then, rather quickly, the media lost interest; there were few follow-ups. Only one paper kept the story alive: the local *Home News*.

This was hardly surprising. The *Home News* had a large stake in the outcome. Just as the 1935 story by the *World Telegram*'s Frederick E. Woltman had first brought the Bergel case to national attention, so, too, the sensational report by Peter Parisi had resurrected the affair exactly fifty years later.

On the basis of Parisi's allegations, the *Home News* adopted an instant and unwavering editorial stand. Bergel had been fired "because he refused to participate in a pro-Nazi propaganda program." His dismissal had been based "on what history has shown to be trumped-up charges." And the man most responsible for this outrage, Friedrich J. Hauptmann, had "later worked in Czechoslovakia for Joseph Goebbels, the Nazi propaganda minister." With these "facts" now clearly established, the *Home News* asked Rutgers to "clear the record with an apology for injustice by a previous administration."[1]

These stories and editorials had a powerful effect. They created the climate that led university officials to set up our committee. In a real sense, the *Home News* was the agent that reignited this case; Alan Silver merely supplied the fuel.

Why was the *Home News* so interested in Bergel's cause? There are a number of possible answers. His case was timely, the setting was local, the subject was intriguing. Parisi's first story coincided with President Reagan's visit to the Bitburg cemetery, where members of the infamous S.S. are buried. Perhaps the *Home News* was trying to right an old wrong, as it said, though its record in such matters is hardly impressive. Perhaps personal motives played a role. The reporter who broke the story has privately expressed his bitterness about personnel policies at Rutgers.[2]

Following our press conference, the *Home News* ran two more editorials on the case. The first one observed that our Interim Report would neither "comfort" Lienhard Bergel nor "satisfy" Alan Silver. The second claimed that "something" was missing. "At the end of all the reviews and the explanations, it is impossible to overlook what happened: Bergel, the outspoken Nazi critic, lost his job and the university went out of its way to defend Nazi apologist Hauptmann. And for that—for the way the university treated Lienhard Bergel—an apology is still in order."[3]

President Bloustein disagreed. In his view, Rutgers had honored its pledge to provide a historical assessment of the case. With that assessment (or Interim Report) now readily available, Bloustein invited interested readers to draw their own conclusions. The *Home News* did not think this was enough; it responded with several articles about the Interim Report and its critics. Featured was Alan Silver, who cited numerous "flaws" in our "whitewash." When Silver was unavailable for comment, the *Home News* quoted his neighbors or simply manufactured a story.

One such example occurred in January 1987. Under the headline, "Prof Wants to Debate Bergel Report Authors," Parisi began:

A Rutgers University professor wants to debate the authors of [the Bergel Report]. . . . But the head of the panel has declined the challenge, at least for now.

Contending that the report contains "major omissions, major distortions," Sol Chaneles, associate professor of administration of justice, yesterday issued the challenge through the staff of the campus newspaper, *The Daily Targum*.[4]

What Parisi failed to mention was his own role in creating this story. It was he who spoke to Silver and Chaneles about setting up the debate. It was he who alerted the campus newspaper. And it was he who reported our refusal to accept the "challenge" that he himself had largely invented.*

At about this point, we decided to meet with the *Home News* editors. We were particularly interested in the paper's current position on Parisi's early articles. We wondered whether the editors were aware of the crucial errors, exaggerations, and omissions. Would they be angry or embarrassed? Would they defend Parisi? Would they care at all? The answers, it turned out, were as disturbing as the articles themselves.

We met at the *Home News* offices. Editor Richard Hughes was there, along with his chief aides and the paper's ombudsman. We asked the group to consider the headline of Parisi's first article: "Nazi spy, FBI aide principals in 1935 controversy at RU." The headline was false. After eighteen months of digging, we have found no evidence that Hauptmann had been a Nazi spy or that

---

* Professor Chaneles, one of Parisi's major "sources," never produced the "omissions" and "distortions" he claimed to have found. This was hardly surprising. A few months later, the *New York Times* reported that five paintings presently owned by New York's Metropolitan Museum of Art had been confiscated by the Nazis from Jewish families in Europe. The sole source for this story was Mr. Chaneles, who strongly suggested that the Metropolitan had acquired the paintings illegally. The following day, however, the *Times* retracted the entire story ("Records at the Met Disprove Charge of Acquiring 5 Paintings Improperly"). Clearly embarrassed, the *Times* quoted the angry director, who said: "None of the allegations about the five paintings has any basis in fact. I am sorry that Chaneles's amateur investigations have been taken seriously." See *New York Times*, Nov. 24, 25, 1987.

Bergel had worked for the FBI. This posed no problem for the editors; one of them explained that headlines were meant to grab the reader's attention, nothing more.

We turned next to the substance of Parisi's article. The second paragraph began: "The story involves a department chairman who turned out to be a Nazi spy and a faculty member who turned into a temporary part-time FBI operative." This was a categorical statement, not a headline. Again, the staff sensed no problem. We must understand, said the editors, that Parisi had gotten his information from "sources." The fact that he did not verify this information, or use quotation marks, or even attribute it, was unimportant. Parisi was only reporting what others had told him.

There was no way to pierce this airtight defense. Each time we brought up an error in one of Parisi's articles, the editors referred to "sources." Sadly, they did not say much about journalistic responsibility—the responsibility to check facts, to report events accurately, and to retract obvious mistakes.

Still, the conference may have changed some minds. A few weeks later, the *Home News* ran a story by Parisi headlined "Rutgers Firing Case Will Not Be Laid to Rest." But that seemed to end the crusade; there were no sequels, no more blasts by Alan Silver, no more calls for apologies or debates. Perhaps not coincidentally, Parisi left the *Home News* to take a teaching position in Pennsylvania.[5]

On December 13, 1987, Bergel was struck by a car near his home on Long Island. He died two days later, at the age of 81. According to Sylvia Bergel, her husband had hoped to be remembered for his scholarly achievements, not for his troubles in New Brunswick. Nevertheless, she added, "Alan Silver and I are continuing our efforts to have Rutgers disavow its support of Hauptmann, and withdraw its personal and professional attacks on Lienhard Bergel, as published in the Trustees Report of 1935."[6]

The *Home News* marked Bergel's passing with a photo and a front-page story. Though the sub-headline was badly mangled—it read "Lienhard Bergel fired for *alleged* anti Nazi views . . ." when it meant "Lienhard Bergel *allegedly* fired for anti-Nazi views"— the story itself was professional in every respect. Reporter Hanelle

Rubin had carefully checked the facts. Sources were clearly identified. The circumstances leading to Bergel's termination were
thoughtfully presented. In what may have been its final word on the
case, the *Home News* had played the story straight.[7]

The same could be said of the AAUP. Early on, the local
chapter had embraced Bergel's cause, honored Alan Silver, and
even appointed the ubiquitous Professor Chaneles to "monitor" our
committee. What that meant was anyone's guess. When Chaneles
submitted his report to the chapter, it was "received" (and buried)
without comment. Despite repeated requests, it has not been made
public.

In the end, the AAUP adopted a cautious resolution on the
case. While praising Bergel for his courage in denouncing Nazism,
as our committee had done, it did not challenge the reasons for his
dismissal or claim that his academic freedom had been violated.
As for an apology, the resolution said nothing at all.[8]

Has "the case of the Nazi professor" been resolved? Probably
not. While we have tried to present all the relevant material, we
can hardly lay claim to omniscience or infallibility. Least of all can
we pretend to be certain about the motivations of the main actors in
this drama.

We do believe, however, that there were plausible reasons for
Bergel to be told by university officials in 1933 that he would not
be retained. What influence Bergel's political differences with
Hauptmann may have had on this decision remains problematical.
The manner in which the whole affair was handled by the University surely is open to criticism, especially in light of current policies and, perhaps, with our present knowledge of Hauptmann's
later career. We could be equally critical of the way the case was
treated by the press, which played up the "newsworthy" elements,
real and fabricated, while ignoring almost everything else. Such vital considerations as the three-year rule, the preference for Emil
Jordan, the impact of the Depression on enrollments and finances,
and the disdain Bergel showed for his collegial duties make tedious
reading, to be sure. But historians and journalists practice different
crafts, and we must treat the dull as well as the spectacular. Nevertheless, whether the reader relies on journalism or history, the final
judgment is his own.

Summary of Findings

(1) Lienhard Bergel was appointed as an instructor in the German Department at the New Jersey College for Women in 1932. The decision to terminate his appointment as of June 30, 1935, was based on a number of important factors. One was economic. The Great Depression of the 1930s had an enormous impact on higher education in New Jersey. In 1933 Rutgers University suffered a reduction of 20 percent in its state appropriation. Enrollments were declining; the future looked bleak.

The economic factor was compounded by an administrative one. In 1933 the University instituted the so-called "three-year rule." If an instructor was not deemed eligible for promotion to assistant professor within three years, his appointment would ordinarily be terminated. This meant that an instructorship was now viewed as a probationary appointment: some would advance; others would not. The German Department had two instructors at this time, Emil Jordan and Lienhard Bergel.

Whether they liked it or not, Jordan and Bergel were competing for promotion to assistant professor. Given the budget cuts and the declining enrollments, there was no chance that both men would be retained. The administration's preference was decidedly for Jordan. He was an able teacher; he played an active role in extracurricular activities on campus; and he was completing a textbook, which received fine reviews upon publication in 1935. Bergel was also a good teacher, although some students criticized his classroom methods. He was not very involved in extra-curricular activities, however, and he had no publications to his credit. Furthermore, Bergel was the junior member of the department, the last one to be hired.

The basic decision to choose Jordan over Bergel was made at the end of the 1932–1933 academic year. It was communicated verbally to Bergel in September 1933 and reaffirmed in writing by Dean Corwin in May 1934. Bergel was given ample notice—far more notice, in fact, than was recommended by the guidelines of the American Association of University Professors. In view of these circumstances, and the need to terminate one member of the German Department, it was entirely plausible for university authorities to favor the retention and promotion of Emil Jordan.

(2) Political considerations probably played a role in this decision. Certainly Bergel and Hauptmann disagreed strongly about the merits of the Hitler regime. No member of the German Department other than Bergel adopted an outspoken anti-Nazi stance. However, there is no evidence that Bergel made the charge of political discrimination until late in 1934; there is no evidence that he raised this issue with Albert Meder, Dean Corwin, or even Professor William Braun. Of course, Hauptmann never accepted the validity of this charge. Had he wanted to do so, Hauptmann probably could have dismissed Bergel after his first year at N.J.C. Yet he seems to have raised no objections to Bergel's remaining for the full three-year term, and—according to his own account—actually encouraged Dean Meder to give Bergel two year's notice instead of one. The committee believes that Hauptmann was clearly biased against Bergel because of his political beliefs, and that this factor could have influenced the decision to favor Jordan over Bergel. However, we believe that the other factors, stated above, were no less consequential in determining the outcome.

(3) A clash of personalities was also an ingredient in the Bergel-Hauptmann relationship. Hauptmann was bluff, domineering, and theatrical. He could also be generous and compassionate, as well as improvident. He was socially and academically insecure and wary of any subordinate who seemed to threaten his status. Bergel described himself as a "bookworm," an intellectual whose academic qualifications were far superior to those of his colleagues. He was anti-authoritarian, stubborn in his convictions, and strongly inclined to place his own interpretation on matters that affected him personally. Bergel had little respect for Hauptmann, who no

doubt felt challenged by the arrogance of this young instructor. It is quite possible that these personal differences set the two men apart even more than their divergent views on Hitler's Germany.

(4) Bergel was never charged with "incompetence" by any university official, despite his assertions to the contrary. Why, then, did he use the term so frequently? In the German academic tradition, as Bergel explained it, a teacher could be discharged only for "incompetence," and only after receiving the opportunity to hear and rebut the charges against him. In Bergel's mind, the same rules applied in America—hence his refusal to accept any notice of termination until these rules were followed. Bergel did not seem to understand that instructors held only one-year appointments, and that no reasons had to be given when such appointments were terminated. Nor did he understand the implications of the three-year rule, which meant that by July 1935 he had to be promoted or let go. In retrospect, the University's great mistake was its failure to inform Bergel of his status in the clear and unmistakable terms that Acting Dean Meder had used in his letter to Professor William Braun in October 1933.

(5) Bergel charged that Hauptmann had used his classroom to preach Nazi doctrines and to disseminate propaganda. There obviously is some truth to this allegation, although student witnesses differed widely in describing the content and amount of the "propaganda" they heard. One point is clear, however: Hauptmann did take time in his language classes to rebut what he characterized as "lies" in American newspapers about conditions in Germany. Some sources have contended that the decline in German enrollments was caused by the students' disapproval of pro-Nazi preachments. This theory is difficult to assess. On the one hand, enrollments in the French Department dropped in about the same proportion as enrollments in the German Department. On the other hand, the ratio of Jewish students in German courses certainly declined in this period—a fact that may signify a distaste for things German, a special antipathy to Hauptmann, or perhaps both.

(6) In disseminating pro-Nazi propaganda pamphlets, Hauptmann appears to have been naive as well as inept. He furnished Professor Van Dorn with German propaganda pamphlets, knowing

full well that Van Dorn loathed the Hitler regime and would certainly present these pamphlets in anything but a sympathetic manner. Furthermore, one may ask what Hauptmann expected to gain by leaving a stack of the infamous Campbell pamphlets in a public area at the very time he had come under attack for distributing pro-Nazi propaganda. It seems likely—in this instance, at least—that Hauptmann was guilty of absentmindedness rather than malevolence.

(7) Although Hauptmann rarely discussed the Nazi regime in public forums, his political views were well known on campus. He was appalled by the Versailles Treaty, hostile to the Weimar constitution, and thrilled by the rise of Adolf Hitler. Hauptmann and his wife made frequent trips to Germany; they arranged for their two daughters to be educated there. In 1935 Hauptmann returned to his "old beloved Marburg" to secure a doctorate with suspicious haste; on the same trip, he boasted of meeting with Nazi officials in Berlin. Five years later, when forced to choose between his "conflicting loyalties," Hauptmann fled to Germany.

(8) The issue of Hauptmann's anti-Semitism must also be addressed. (Bergel, it should be understood, was not a Jew.) Could an enthusiastic admirer of Adolf Hitler fail to embrace the Fuehrer's hatred of the Jews? There is abundant evidence that Hauptmann had friendly relations with Jewish students. He hired them to tutor his children, to do secretarial work in the German Department, and to replace him when he was on leave in Marburg. Jewish students spoke frequently of their affection for Hauptmann, and there is no evidence that he discriminated against anyone in the distribution of grades. Nevertheless, Hauptmann made no secret of his belief that Polish Jews did not belong in Germany, and he rarely criticized Hitler's racial policies. In short, Hauptmann did not appear to be obsessed with this issue in 1935. Whether this appearance was authentic is impossible to prove. During his wartime service in Bratislava, he was not a fanatical racialist. Still, he followed the orders of his superiors there and publicly adhered to the Nazi line on the "Jewish Question."

(9) The behavior of the Rutgers authorities toward Bergel in 1935 and after is questionable in many respects. President

Clothier, Dean Corwin, and former Dean Meder were obviously annoyed by Bergel's persistent refusal to accept his termination, by
his "disloyalty" in seeking the aid of influential state officials, and
by his derogatory remarks about the quality of the German Department. At the hearings in 1935, these officials and their chosen
trustees went out of their way to defend Hauptmann and to repel
Bergel's various charges. Scores of witnesses were allowed to testify, but the questions addressed to them, and the statements made
by Clothier, Corwin, and Meder, reveal an obvious bias against
Bergel. This was hardly surprising, because the University itself
was on trial, accused of being "soft" on Nazism; and it responded
defensively.

In the following years, university officials continued their
questionable activities. They kept Mrs. Hauptmann on the payroll
a year after her job was supposed to be terminated. They refused to
write recommendations for Bergel, who desperately needed a job.
And they secretly aided Hauptmann's attempts to avoid bankruptcy
at a time when they routinely accepted the resignations of other
faculty members who were in financial distress.

The list goes on. In 1940 Corwin and Clothier concealed the
information they had discovered about Hauptmann's likely flight to
Germany. Their objective, once again, was to protect the University from unfavorable publicity. When the matter was revived
in 1946, with the news of Hauptmann's arrest in Austria, President Clothier took the position that the case had been closed for
good by the acceptance of the Ashmead Report. He refused to do
anything more.

(10) Because of his prominent role in reviving interest in the
Bergel-Hauptmann case in 1985, it is appropriate to notice the part
played by Alan Silver in 1935. Then a senior at Rutgers, he was
the head of the local unit of the National Student League, a left-
wing organization that interested itself in Bergel's cause. In May
1935, when it seemed that all efforts to persuade the university authorities to retain Bergel had failed, Silver went into action. By an
acknowledged bluff, he induced President Clothier to talk with
Bergel, a meeting that was to lead to the hearing by the trustees. It
was Silver who contacted the *World Telegram* reporter who first

broke the Bergel-Hauptmann story to the public. And it was Silver who was responsible for bringing the American Civil Liberties Union into the case. It is unlikely that there would have been a "Bergel-Hauptmann case" in 1935 had it not been for the intervention of Alan Silver. For whatever reasons, he did not refer to his own involvement when he reopened the case fifty years later.*

(11) In 1985 the newspapers contained spectacular allegations that Hauptmann had engaged in subversive activities during his years at N.J.C. The committee has found no evidence to support the charges that Hauptmann was involved in espionage of any kind; that he attempted to organize Nazi cells on the campus; or that Joseph Goebbels appointed him "leader of the Germans" in central New Jersey. Furthermore, there is no evidence that Hauptmann belonged to the Friends of New Germany, the German-American Bund, or any other pro-Nazi organization. The source for these accusations against Hauptmann was Lienhard Bergel.

(12) The flight of Hauptmann and his family to Germany was triggered by a confrontation with Dean Corwin in October 1940. As he understood it, she told him that he must make a choice between adopting a "pro-English" position or resigning. His wife, who was still a German citizen, urged that they return to Germany to avoid the kind of experience they had undergone in 1935. As an American citizen, Hauptmann could not get a passport. The German Consul in New York provided him with funds and an alien passport, and he travelled by way of San Francisco through Japan, Korea, and Russia to Germany. His wife and daughter, using German passports, went by ship to Spain, and then to Germany.

(13) It has been alleged that Hauptmann was "a leading propaganda agent in Hitler's blatantly anti-Semitic Propaganda Ministry headed by the notorious Joseph Goebbels." The facts do not sustain this characterization. Hauptmann was a Nazi. He joined the Party in April 1941, soon after his return to Germany. He was employed by the *Deutsche Akademie* (German Academy) as the "national leader" of that institution in Slovakia, a German puppet state created in 1939. Although the Academy after December 1941

---

* Alan Silver died in the spring of 1988 as this book was going to press.

was ostensibly under Goebbel's Propaganda Ministry, the branches outside Germany—such as the one in Slovakia—were assigned to the jurisdiction of the Foreign Office. Hauptmann's propaganda activities were minimal; they consisted of several talks about conditions in America. He was not a member of any of the numerous radical Nazi organizations. Imprisoned and interrogated after the war, he was never prosecuted or charged with any offenses. He sought to return to the United States, but his citizenship was revoked and he was not permitted to immigrate. He remained in Austria and died in obscurity on December 29, 1978.

Notes

1. PROLOGUE

1. The official report of the special trustees' committee that heard the case, entitled, "In the Matter of the Investigation of the Charges of Lienhard Bergel," was published as *Rutgers University Bulletin*, Series XII, No. 2-B, in August 1935 (New Brunswick, N.J., 1935). The *New York Times* alone carried thirty news stories related to the case between May and October 1935.

2. Irene Virag in *Newsday*, September 16, 1985; Michele Landsberg in the *Toronto Globe and Mail*, November 9, 1985. Landsberg added that while the investigation was under way in 1935, "headlines flamed with news of Hitler's violent persecution of Jews. Beside these flamboyant horror stories ran polite reports of Rutgers professors who publicly praised Hitler."

3. New Brunswick *Home News*, May 8, June 11, 1985. On June 11 the *Home News* also ran a letter from Mrs. Sylvia Bergel, which asserted that her husband's dismissal "was based on his refusal to participate in Nazi propaganda activities in the classrooms." She claimed, too, that Hauptmann was Hitler's "vice-gauleiter for Southern Moravia (Czechoslovakia)."

4. *Newsday*, September 16, 1985.

5. *Daily Targum* (Rutgers student newspaper), September 19, 1985; *Toronto Globe and Mail*, November 9, 1985.

6. *Home News*, May 16, 1985.

7. Alan Silver to Edward J. Bloustein, June 11, 1935, in Committee File. Silver was also critical of "the inaccurate and pro-administration account" in Richard P. McCormick's *Rutgers: A Bicentennial History* (New Brunswick, 1966), pp. 238–239, to which Bloustein had referred in his statement.

8. Edward J. Bloustein to Alan Silver, July 1, 1985, in Committee File.

9. Alan Silver to Jack Wysoker, July 10, 1985; Silver to Lienhard and Sylvia Bergel, July 10, 1985, in Committee File; *Home News*, July 24, 1985; *Daily Targum*, September 19, 1985; Silver to Bloustein, July 22, 26, 1985, in Committee File. In his letter of July 22, Silver warned Bloustein "that the forces now set in motion, absent some change in your position, will inevitably result in exposing Rutgers University to some very damaging public relations."

10. *Home News*, September 25, 29, 1985; *Newark Star Ledger*, September 25, 27, 1985; *New York Times*, September 8, 1985.

11. *Newsday*, September 16, 1985.

12. Sylvia Bergel to Edward J. Bloustein, September 12, 1985, in Committee File.

2. THE DECISION

1. Relevant background information on Rutgers University in this period will be found in Richard P. McCormick, *Rutgers: A Bicentennial History* (New Brunswick, 1966), especially chapters 9 and 10, and George Schmidt, *Douglass College: A History* (New Brunswick, 1968).

2. The last meeting of the university faculty was held on June 7, 1933. Under new "Rules and Regulations" adopted by the Rutgers trustees on October 18, 1933, there was no provision for a faculty body at the university level. Trustee Minutes, October 18, 1933. The best source on personnel policies and procedures can be found in the material assembled in 1943–1944 by the Committee on Personnel Procedures, whose work resulted in extensive reforms. See *Faculty News Letter*, August, October, November 1944, and January 1945. Not until 1937 was it specified that assistant professors were to be appointed for three-year renewable terms, with the understanding that they would "resign on request in event of financial necessity or other good reason." Trustee Minutes, April 9, 1937. Unless otherwise noted, all source materials cited are in the University-Archives, Alexander Library, Rutgers University.

3. The state appropriation for the whole university fell from $1,034,533 in 1931–1932 to $747,860 in 1933–1934. The allocation for N.J.C. was reduced from $402,428 to $272,160. For details on budgetary conditions, see *The Report of the President of Rutgers University*, published annually in October by the University. Prior to the budget cuts, the trustees had as a goal the implementation of a salary scale with minima of $2,000 for instructors, $3,000 for assistant professors, $4,000 for associate professors, and $5,000 for full professors, but the goal was not achieved until after 1945. On this matter, and on the reluctance to grant promotions without increases in salary, see Dean Walter T. Marvin to President Robert C. Clothier, Trustee Papers, April 17, 1936. Clothier noted that normal faculty promotions had been held back for five years because of inadequate funds and said that he tried to handle the "morale factor" by individual conferences with those who merited promotion.

4. Official enrollment figures are given in the annual *Report of the President*. The enrollment at N.J.C. did not rise above a thousand again until the academic year 1939–1940, when it reached 1,044. It should be noted here that enrollment figures in different sources may vary slightly, depending on the specific time during the year when they are calculated. October counts, for example, will usually not correspond with those made at the start of classes in September.

5. On the early years of N.J.C., see Schmidt, *Douglass College*, chapters 1 and 11, and McCormick, *Rutgers*, chapters 8 and 9.

6. Material about Hauptmann's background can be found in Friedrich J. Hauptmann Personnel File, Douglass College Archives.

7. *Ibid.* For the path taken by German ex-veterans like Hauptmann, see Michael Kater, *Studentschaft und Rechtsradikalismus in Deutschland, 1918–1933* (Hamburg, 1975), especially pp. 20, 35, 102, 124 for the University of Marburg; Stephen Steinberg, *Sabers and Brownshirts: The German Students' Path to National Socialism, 1918–1933* (Chicago, 1977), pp. 21–86. For a superb account of the adoption of National Socialism in Marburg, see Rudy Koshar, *Bourgeois Marburg, 1880–1935: Social Life, Local Politics, and Nazism* (Chapel Hill, N.C., 1987).

8. In 1931 Hauptmann was requested to return his ordination papers as assistant pastor of the Emanuel Lutheran Church in New York. The stated reason was Hauptmann's "consistent failure to attend church or communion." During the trustees' hearings, Hauptmann claimed that "I have, at the end of that matter, received a very kind letter from the president of the New York Synod which says that if I ever would like to be again ordained there would be not the slightest objection." See *Daily Home News*, June 3, 1931, June 7, 1935. The question of whether Hauptmann was *forced* to leave Gettysburg College cannot be definitively answered. Charles E. Glassick, the current president of Gettysburg, wrote to our committee on November 18, 1985: "Unfortunately we do not have faculty folders from that era and so are unable to be specific regarding the reasons for Hauptmann leaving Gettysburg College. . . . It does appear to me that Hauptmann simply served on the faculty for a few years and then moved on in keeping with the President's policy at that time." Charles E. Glassick to David Oshinsky, November 18, 1985, copy in committee's possession. Furthermore, when the American Civil Liberties Union claimed, in 1935, that Hauptmann may have been dismissed from Gettysburg for spreading political propaganda, the president of Gettysburg, Henry W. Hanson, responded with a blistering telegram. It read: "Received Report of Hauptmans (sic) Dismissal For Engaging in Political Propaganda. Ridiculous. Professor Hauptmann Resigned. Never At Any Time Was He Even Questioned Or Suspected Of Any Political Propaganda." See Henry A. Hanson to Lucille Millner, May 18, 1935, ACLU File, Rutgers University Archives.

9. Data on course schedules and enrollments, not always consistent, can be found in Record Group (RG) #19/A/0/1 (Douglass College—Records of the Dean), Box 32, f., "Enrollments, 1932–52," and f. "Statistics, 1934–1937." From the peak in 1931–1932, German enrollments declined in succeeding years to 272 (1932–1933), 270 (1933–1934), 218 (1934–1935), and 196 (1935–1936), according to a compilation made by Esther Hawes, Registrar, on April 8, 1936. See f. "Statistics, 1934–1937. Total college enrollments declined over the same period from 1,074 to 949. On the personnel of the German Department, see the individual personnel files, Douglass College Archives, and the *Rutgers University Bulletin*, Series XII, No. 2-B (August 1935), pp. 4, 7–9, cited hereafter as "Trustees' Committee Report."

10. Robert C. Clothier in *Report of the President . . . 1933–34*, p. 7.

11. "Trustees Committee Report," pp. 5–7; Statement of Albert E. Meder, [1935], Box 4, f., "Administration Statements by Officials," hereafter cited as Meder Statement, 1935. Correspondence and other documents relevant to the hearing conducted by the Special Trustee Committee can be found in Record Group #3/CO/2 in the Rutgers University Archives, Alexander Library. They are filed in labelled folders in five boxes. Subsequent citations of sources in this record group will refer only to the box number and the folder designation. See also Alice Schlimbach and Emil Jordan, "The German House: A Successful Educational Experiment in Modern Language Teaching on a College Campus," *The Modern Language Journal* 20 (March 1936), pp. 357–352, which makes quite clear the emphasis placed on giving students a feeling for German "culture."

12. On Zoller, see Meder Statement, 1935, p. 2; "Trustees Committee Report," p. 14. Professor Manuel Salas of the Spanish Department stated in 1935 that he was prepared to testify that the administration was fully justified in the decision made regarding Miss Zoller. Salas to Clothier, Box 1, f., "Communications to Committee—Resolutions of Organizations."

13. Biographical material on Bergel can be found in Lienhard Bergel Personnel File, Douglass College Archives. Dean Douglass was initially reluctant to make this third change in instructors because of the adverse effect it could have on the students. She decided, despite Miss Cook's pressure for hasty action, that Bergel's credentials should be obtained and verified before she agreed to his appointment. Bergel was appointed for the remainder of the academic year and was informed that his salary for 1932–1933 would be $1,800 "should the position prove to your satisfaction and your work satisfactory to us." For the relevant correspondence, see Sylvia Cook to Professor Julian Moreno-Lacalle, [November], 1931; Lacalle to Dean Mabel S. Douglass, November 6, 1931; Douglass to Moreno-Lacalle, November 12, 1931; Moreno-Lacalle to Douglass, November 16, 1931; Douglass to Lienhard Bergel, December 12, 1931; Bergel to Douglass, February 3, 1932, in Box 2, f., "Committee Hearings, Exhibits, Committee Exhibits." Moreno-Lacalle was the executive officer of the short-lived Division of Language and Literature at N.J.C.

14. Bergel's testimony, Book 8, pp. 288–289, Book 7, p. 151. During the course of the investigation conducted by the trustees' committee, an estimated 1,342,000 words of testimony from 110 witnesses were recorded in shorthand by an expert stenographer. A typed transcription would have run to 5,328 pages. At the request of the committee, only a small portion of the testimony was actually transcribed. It amounted to 785 pages, contained in eight separate binders, or "books." Over 400 pages, to be found in books 1, 7, and 8, contain testimony given by Bergel; the rest is devoted to selected student and faculty witnesses. See Box 2, fs. 15–18; Box 3, fs. 1–2, "Committee Hearings, Stenographic Record and Transcripts." All subsequent citations of the transcripts will give merely the identity of the person giving the testimony, the book, and the page numbers. See also Bergel's statement transmitted to President Clothier through Harry S. Feller, March 1935, p. 2 (hereafter cited as Bergel Statement, March 1935), Box 4, f.,

"Administration—Statements by Officials"; Sylvia Bergel to Dean Margaret T. Corwin, October 1, 1934, Box 3, f. 2, "Committee Hearings, Exhibits, Committee Exhibits"; Meder Statement, 1935, p. 3; "Trustees' Committee Report," p. 42.

15. The best account of pro-Nazi activities in the United States and the reactions they provoked, is Sander A. Diamond, *The Nazi Movement in the United States, 1924–1941* (Ithaca, N.Y., 1974). For American press coverage of Nazi anti-Semitism, and the reactions it provoked, see Deborah Lipstadt, *Beyond Belief: The American Press and the Coming of the Holocaust, 1933–1945* (New York, 1986), especially chs. 1–3.

16. On the status of Jews in Germany under Hitler there is a vast literature, but a useful survey is Karl A. Schleunes, *The Twisted Road to Auschwitz: Nazi Policy Toward German Jews, 1933–1938* (Urbana, Ill., 1970).

17. *Campus News*, February 16, April 29, October 7, 1932. See also the interview with Sylvia Cook, *ibid.*, December 11, 1931. *Targum*, December 7, 1932. See also *ibid.*, March 18, 1933, for similar statements by Professor Holzmann.

18. Jordan's talk was reported in the *Campus News*, March 31, 1933, and in the (New Brunswick) *Daily Home News*, March 30, 1933. Sylvia Bergel also participated in the discussion and reported that while she was in Breslau as a student she had been "hit over the head" by a Nazi. See Evelyn Lehman Testimony, Book 6, p. 26. There was intense public interest at this time because of the imminence of the scheduled boycott of Jewish businesses in Germany. It was evidently at about this time that Hauptmann called the members of the department together and cautioned them to be careful what they said about affairs in Germany until reliable information was available. See, "Trustees' Committee Report" (known as Final Report), p. 39.

19. Bergel's participation is not mentioned in either of the newspaper accounts, but it is referred to in several other sources. See, Bergel Statement, March 1935, pp. 3–4; Statement of Lienhard Bergel, May 1935, (hereafter cited as Bergel Statement, May 1935), p. 4, Box 4, f., "Bergel and Counsel."

20. There are reports on this meeting in the *Daily Home News*, March 30, 1933, and in *Targum*, April 1, 1933. Prior to the meeting, consideration had been given to adopting a resolution protesting against acts of anti-Semitism in Germany, but this plan was not carried out. *Ibid.*, March 25, 1933.

21. On the status of Polish Jews in Germany, see Donald L. Niewyk, *The Jews in Weimar Germany* (Baton Rouge, La., 1980), pp. 15–17, 114–121.

22. *Targum*, April 1, 1933. See the exchange of letters between Carl Weiss and Charles Brodsky, *ibid.*, April 1, 4, 1933.

23. *Daily Home News*, March 30, 1933.

24. *Ibid.*, April 1, 1933.

25. *Targum*, May 3, 1933; *Daily Home News*, May 24, 25, June 6, 1933. In 1936 Holzmann and his German-born wife led a tour group to Germany to attend the Olympic Games. See *New Brunswick Sunday Times*, April 1, 1936.

26. Minutes, Trustees' Executive Committee, February 4, 1933. Instructors were a numerous group at that period. In 1933, of 87 full-time faculty at N.J.C.,

27 were at the rank of instructor, 29 were assistant professors, 15 were associate professors, and 15 were full professors. Because of budgetary and enrollment constraints in 1933, few of the instructors could anticipate promotions. Former Acting-Dean Meder stated in May 1935, that of 10 instructors appointed during 1931–1932, 3 were still on the staff and none had been promoted. Because the three-year rule did not take effect until July 1, 1932, no instructors were subject to automatic termination before June 30, 1935. Meder Statement, 1935, p. 6.

27. *Ibid.*, p. 4.

28. Dean Douglass became ill in the spring of 1932 and was granted a year's leave of absence. She died on September 21, 1932. Albert E. Meder, a member of the Mathematics Department was appointed Acting-Dean as of September 15, 1932, and served until Margaret T. Corwin assumed the deanship on February 1, 1934. The main account of Meder's conference with Hauptmann is in Meder Statement, 1935, pp. 6–8. It was Hauptmann's recollection in 1935 that it had first been decided that Bergel should receive only a year's notice, but that he had suggested two years because the Bergels were grieving the loss of their first child. Statement by F. J. Hauptmann, [May, 1935], Box 3, f., "Committee Hearings—Statements gotten from Stenographer," p. 2, cited hereafter as Hauptmann Statement, May, 1935.

29. "Excerpts from Mrs. Bergel's Notebook, 1933," Box 2, f., "Committee Hearings, Exhibits, Bergel Exhibits, 25–51; Clothier to L. Bergel, June 24, 1935, in *ibid.*; Bergel's testimony, Book 7, pp. 1–4.

30. This conversation is reported in Hauptmann Statement, May 1935, p. 3; Bergel Statement, March 1935, p. 4; Bergel Statement, May 1935, p. 1; and Bergel's testimony, Book 7, pp. 4–5.

31. Reports on this conversation are in the Meder Statement, 1935, p. 8; Bergel Statement, March 1935, p. 4; Bergel Statement, May 1935, p. 1. In neither of these statements did Bergel indicate that he had told Meder that Hauptmann's attitude toward him was the result of political bias, but he did make such a charge in his later oral testimony. Bergel's testimony, Book 7, p. 12, Book 8, p. 287.

32. Bergel's testimony, Book 7, pp. 14–15; W. A. Braun to Meder, October 26, 1933; Meder to Braun, October 30, 1933, both in Box 2, f., "Committee Hearings—Exhibits, Committee Exhibits." There was no hint in Braun's letter that Bergel had alleged that his political differences with Hauptmann were the source of the problem.

33. In the course of his testimony before the trustees' committee, Bergel first stated that his wife's message from Braun was that he did not have to "worry about his position for the next year." Moments later, he changed his position to "did not have to worry about his position." What Braun actually told Mrs. Bergel and what she told her husband cannot now be ascertained, but the discrepancy in the two versions of the message is critical. It would appear from his testimony that Bergel accepted the second version, which was not at all in accord with Meder's letter. See Bergel's testimony, Book 7, pp. 15–16; *ibid.*, Book 8, pp. 299–303, 392–

397. Bergel said that Braun showed him Meder's letter in the summer of 1934. *Ibid.*, Book 8, p. 303.

34. *Ibid.*, Book 7, p. 48. It may also be relevant that both Bergel and his wife seem to have had the impression that his position was to be "permanent" if both he and the College were mutually satisfied. Bergel Statement, March 1935, p. 1. It is true that there were no limitations on the number of years an instructor might serve at the time of Bergel's appointment, but the "three-year rule" altered the situation.

35. See the "Statement" adopted on January 2, 1925, at a joint conference of the American Association of University Professors and other major educational organizations in Walter P. Metzger, ed., *The American Concept of Academic Freedom in Formation* (New York, 1977), pp. 100–102. Not until 1971, after considerable discussion, did the AAUP endorse the position that probationary faculty should be given reasons for termination, and then only in the event that the faculty member requested them. See "Statement on Procedural Standards in the Renewal or Non-renewal of Faculty Appointments," 1971, *ibid.*, following page 446. A copy of the 1925 statement was sent to the president of Rutgers in 1927 by the chairman of the Commission on Academic Freedom and Academic Tenure of the Association of American Colleges. With it was a request that the president submit the statement to the Board of Trustees and report on any action. There is no indication that any response was made. See Clothier Papers, 134–8A, f., "Academic Tenure."

3. THE DECISION REAFFIRMED

1. *Report of the President . . . 1934–1935, passim;* Clothier to Deans, December 8, 1933, Clothier Papers, 134–129, f. "A. E. Meder"; Trustee Papers, October 18, 1933; Clothier Papers, 136–159, f., "State Relations, 1933."

2. Schmidt, *Douglass College*, pp. 86–90; *Campus News*, January 10, 1934.

3. *Campus News*, October 21, 1932; May 12, 1934; *Targum*, November 11, 1933.

4. *Targum*, March 10, 17, April 11, 1934; *Campus News*, March 24, 1934. In March students held a mass meeting to condemn the Vinson Naval Appropriation Bill and oppose the construction of an armory on the university campus.

5. For a good account of student radicalism in the 1930s and its relation to the peace movement, see Hal Draper, "The Student Movement of the Thirties: A Political History," in Rita Simon, ed., *As We Saw the Thirties* (Urbana, Ill., 1967), especially pp. 168–72. An important contemporary account by a participant is James Wechsler, *Revolt on the Campus* (New York, 1935). See also, *Targum*, April 18, 1934.

6. For Rudolfs see, *Targum*, October 11, 1933; for Cap, *ibid.*, October 6, 1934 and *Daily Home News*, October 7, 1934; for Clark, *Campus News*, October 21, 1933. Bergel participated in the discussion that followed Clark's lecture and described the German people as "a herd of buffaloes following the leading bull." Hauptmann scolded him for making such a remark about the land of his

birth. Jordan, who was also present at the meeting, told Bergel that his metaphor was in bad taste. See "Trustees' Committee Report," p. 40.

7. The best account of pro-Nazi organizations in the United States is Diamond, *Nazi Movement*. See also, Neil R. McMillen, "Pro-Nazi Sentiment in the United States, March 1933–March 1934." *Southern Quarterly*, 11 (October 1963), pp. 48–70. Also relevant are the admirable studies by John P. Diggins, *Mussolini and Fascism: The View from America* (Princeton, 1972) and Gaetano Salvemini, *Italian Fascist Activities in the United States* (New York, 1977). The work of the McCormack-Dickstein Committee is best described in Walter Goodman, *The Committee: The Extraordinary Career of the House Committee on Un-American Activities* (New York, 1968), chapter 1. For mainstream German-American sentiment, see Frederick Luebke, "The Germans," in John Higham, ed., *Ethnic Leadership in America* (Baltimore, 1978). Not until 1938 did the organizations referred to declare their opposition to Hitler and his policies.

8. Bergel's testimony, Books 1, 7, 8, *passim*. Bergel estimated that he had attended three faculty meetings during his tenure at N.J.C.; a check by an administrative officer at the College indicated that he was present at only one meeting. Bergel stated that he had been told by Hauptmann that he did not need to attend faculty meetings; that they were a waste of time. He added that after receiving notice that he was to be dismissed, he concluded that the College did not want his active participation. He was also of the opinion that attendance at the meetings was low. *Ibid.*, Book 7, pp. 133–145. In actuality, during the years 1931–1935, attendance exceeded two-thirds of the full-time faculty. L. Bergel Personnel File, IV, Douglass College Archives.

9. Hauptmann Statement, 1935, p. 3; Bergel Statement, March 1935, p. 1; Meder Statement, 1935, p. 9. Bergel's testimony, Book 7, pp. 19–20. In his testimony Bergel denied that he had mentioned "high officials," as the source of his assurance. He said he had referred to his wife's report about Meder's letter to Professor Braun: "You don't have to worry about your position." It was not until sometime after this conversation with Hauptmann that Bergel actually saw Meder's letter. *Ibid.*, Book 8, pp. 299–303; 392–397.

10. Meder Statement, 1935, p. 9; Hauptmann Statement, 1935, pp. 3–4.

11. Corwin's "Report to the Trustees Committee," Box 4, f., "Administration—Statements by Officials" (hereafter cited as Corwin Statement, 1935), pp. 5–7.

12. Corwin to Bergel, May 23, 1934, attached as Exhibit C to President Clothier's Statement, May 1935, in Box 4, f., "Administration—Statements by Officials."

13. Corwin to F. J. Hauptmann, June 5, 1934, in F. J. Hauptmann Personnel File, Douglass College Archives.

14. Emil L. Jordan Personnel File, Douglass College Archives. Jordan was promoted to assistant professor in October 1935. He succeeded Hauptmann as department head in 1941, and was advanced to associate professor in 1943 and to professor in 1950. He retired in 1966.

15. Bergel's testimony, Book 7, pp. 23–24.

16. Corwin's Statement, 1935, p. 9; Bergel's testimony, Book 7, pp. 25–27.

17. Sylvia Bergel to Corwin, October 1, 1934, Box 3, f. 2, "Committee Hearings, Exhibits, Committee Exhibits." See also, Bergel's testimony, Book 7, pp. 31–32.

18. Corwin Statement, 1935, p. 9.

19. *Ibid.*, pp. 9–10; Bergel's testimony, Book 7, pp. 27–36; Bergel Statement, March 1935, p. 1. During his interrogation before the Trustees' Special Committee, one questioner pursued the issue of what Hauptmann had told Bergel regarding letters of recommendation. "Did he say he would not give you letters of recommendation, or he would not be able to give you letters of recommendation?" Bergel replied: "I don't see what the difference is." When the questioner said there was a difference, Bergel responded: "He would not give me letters of recommendation. I think that is what he said. . . . I think it was that there would be no letters of recommendation, so far as I can remember." *Ibid.*, pp. 29–30. Evelyn Lehman, an undergraduate who served as a secretary in the German Department in 1934–1935, testified that she saw "several" letters written by Hauptmann in behalf of Bergel. Lehman's testimony, Book 6, pp. 38, 53–54.

20. Bergel's testimony, Book 7, pp. 36–37; Book 8, p. 314.

4. RUMORS

1. Bergel's testimony, Book 7, p. 39; Book 8, pp. 309, 402–404.

2. *Ibid.*, Book 7, p. 59; *Daily Home News*, July 5, June 13, 1935. Bergel also discussed his problems with Professor Selman Waksman and with the two refugee professors, Lassner and Kreutzer. See, Bergel's testimony, Book 8, pp. 326–327. Miss Shapiro, the daughter of a local rabbi, had close relations with Hauptmann. While in Germany, he sought to arrange for her to spend a year in that country with the family of a Jewish rabbi and to bring the rabbi's daughter to America. See the correspondence in Box 2, f., "F. J. Hauptmann Exhibits."

3. Hauptmann to Corwin, June 9, 1934, Bergel Personnel File, Douglass College Archives; Hauptmann Statement, May 1935, p. 4; Corwin Statement, May 1935, p. 7; Trustee Minutes, October 5, 1934. In Hauptmann's absence, Jordan acted as head of the department.

4. Hauptmann to Corwin, November 30, 1934, Hauptmann Personnel File, Douglass College Archives. Hanfstaengl had visited the United States and had caused a sensation by attending the Harvard Commencement in June 1934.

5. For Hanfstaengl's influence in Germany, see Ernst "Putzi" Hanfstaengl, *Hitler: The Missing Years* (London, 1957). For the chaos that pervaded German universities and their lack of objective standards, see Ernst Baeumler, *Politik und Erziehung* (Berlin, 1937); Ernst Krieck, *Nationalpolitische Erziehung* (Osterwieck, 1933); as well as the standard outline of the Nazification process, Karl D. Bracher, *The German Dictatorship* (New York, 1970), pp. 247–272.

6. Hauptmann to Corwin, November 30, 1934, Hauptmann Personnel File, Douglass College Archives. Max Weinreich, the author of an early study on the

Nazification of German universities, claims that Deutschbein was an early adherent of Hitler. See Weinreich, *Hitler's Professors: The Part of Scholarship in Germany's Crimes against the Jewish People* (New York, 1946), p. 15. But Professor Rudy Koshar of UCLA, the author of a comprehensive study on the Nazi conquest of the town of Marburg, disputes Weinreich's claim. Koshar has provided our committee with information that Deutschbein was a long-time member of the German Democratic Party. Koshar's book is entitled *Bourgeois Marburg, 1890–1935: Social Life, Local Politics, and Nazism* (Chapel Hill, N.C., 1987).

7. Friedrich Johannes Hauptmann, *Eine wissenschaftliche Kritik des Standes des deutschen Unterrichts an den High-Schools und Colleges der Vereinigten Staaten* (Marburg, 1937), especially pp. 1, 33. Hauptmann claims to have received responses to his questionnaire from Maine on December 7, Oklahoma on December 17, and Vermont on December 19. Since he did not even begin work on his dissertation until the end of November *at the earliest*, it seems unlikely— given the slowness of transatlantic mail service and the customary delays of state bureaucracies in America—that he could have received his material so quickly. A copy of Hauptmann's dissertation is on file at the Teachers College of Columbia University.

8. *Campus News*, September 12, 26, October 3, 13, 1934; *Targum*, October 10, 1934; Schmidt, *Douglass College*, pp. 98–99.

9. Corwin Statement, May 1935, p. 11. It is possible that these were the letters forwarded by Professor Waksman to Carl R. Woodward, the Secretary of the University. See Box 1, f., "Communications to Committee—Submitting Evidence"; Trustees' Committee Report, p. 44.

10. Clothier Memorandum, undated, Box 4, f., "Harry S. Feller"; Bergel's testimony, Book 8, p. 331.

11. On discrimination against Jews in this period, see Heywood Broun and George Britt, *Christians Only: A Study in Prejudice* (New York, 1931). Conditions at Rutgers are described on pages 112–114. For a recent discussion, see Charles Silberman, *A Certain People: American Jews and their Lives Today* (New York, 1985).

12. There is considerable material on this matter in the Clothier Papers, 134–142, f., "Jews, Discrimination," and in the J. Edward Ashmead Papers, 108–105, f., "Discrimination Against Jews." Ashmead headed the special committee that dealt with the complaint.

13. *Newark News*, March 26, 1932; Bergel Personnel File, IV, doc. 105, Douglass College Archives. Whether the decline in the proportion of Jewish students was due to a general antipathy to Germany or whether it resulted from the pro-Nazi attitudes of members of the German Department is difficult to determine.

14. Broun and Britt, *Christians Only*, pp. 179–187. Silberman states that "American universities were virtually *Judenrein* until after World War II. *A Certain People*, p. 98.

15. Bergel's testimony, Book 7, p. 39; *ibid.*, Book 8, pp. 331, 335. Bergel testified that it was his understanding that Clothier had requested a statement from him; Clothier denied that he had made such a request. Statement of Robert C. Clothier, July 1935, copy #2, Box 4, f., "R. C. Clothier (Cited hereafter as Clothier Statement, July 1935).

16. Bergel Statement, March 1935. The document ran to six single-spaced typed pages.

17. Clothier Statement, July 1935, p. 3; Corwin Statement, May 1935, pp. 11–13. In addition to the two documents, Feller gave Clothier a copy of Sylvia Bergel's letter of October 1, 1934, which had been provided by Bergel to Dean Corwin. The biographical data, headed "Historical Sketch of Members of German Department of New Jersey College for Women," contained inaccuracies and innuendoes obviously intended to reflect unfavorably on the persons described. Although Bergel claimed to know nothing about this document, it is almost certain that he or Mrs. Bergel, or perhaps both, wrote these sketches. See Bergel's testimony, Book 7, pp. 111–120.

18. Clothier to Feller, March 25, 1935, Exhibit G., attached to Clothier Statement, May 1935.

19. On Clothier, see McCormick, *Rutgers*, ch. 10; the brief pamphlet *Robert Clarkson Clothier*, printed by the trustees shortly after his death in 1970, and the *Rutgers Alumni Monthly*, May 1970, pp. 6–9.

20. Bergel's testimony, Book 7, pp. 42–53; *ibid.*, Book 8, pp. 336–338. It is puzzling how the words "investigation" and "incompetence" took root in Bergel's recollection of Waksman's report of Clothier's letter. Waksman had apparently read the letter. Bergel said "he was able to quote sentences from it at that time, and state them rather accurately." *Ibid.*, Book 7, p. 43. Clothier's brief letter did not contain either of the words referred to. Similarly, Clothier's letter to Corwin had asked merely that she "check up on" matters referred to in Bergel's statement.

21. New York *Times*, May 22, August 24, 1934; April 11, 1935.

22. Ch. 151, 155, *Laws of New Jersey*, 1935. The measure had been sponsored in the Assembly by John J. Rafferty of Middlesex County. A similar bill had passed the Assembly unanimously in April 1934, but did not receive Senate approval. There was strong opposition to the measure from the American Civil Liberties Union and Communist groups. *New York Times*, April 18, 22, 24, 1934.

23. Sylvia Bergel to C. E. Loiseaux, April 8, 1935, Box 2, f. 9, "Bergel Exhibits." Loiseaux represented the county in which the Bergels resided. For Bergel's explanation of this letter, see Bergel's testimony, Book 7, p. 53.

24. *Targum*, October 24, 31, 1934. At Rutgers, where both the *Targum* at the men's colleges and the *Campus News* at N.J.C. tended to view the leftward trend with reserve, if not outright hostility, the new mobilization against war and fascism did not attract the support it achieved at Columbia University or at Brooklyn College, for example, but it did enlist the sympathies of hundreds of undergraduates of diverse political orientations.

25. *Targum*, November 4, 1934. Silver recounted how Joseph Lash had come to New Brunswick to ask him to organize a unit of the Student League for Industrial Democracy, but because he found the Young Communists more vigorous, Silver decided to align with the NSL. Silver Interview, November 27, 1985.

26. On the national movement, see Wechsler, *Campus in Rebellion, passim; Targum*, March 3, April 13, 1935; *Campus News*, March 3, 1935. *Targum* was also alarmed by the NSL's activities, which were described in an editorial as threatening the "overthrow of our existing institutions by processes other than orderly," *Targum*, February 2, 1935. The NSL answered these charges by saying that the overwhelming majority of its members were non-Communists, that it was against "imperial wars," and that it was, indeed, opposed to fascism as it was then manifest in Germany.

27. Bergel's testimony, Book 7, pp. 65–67; *ibid.*, Book 8, pp. 366–372; *Daily Home News*, July 10, 1935.

28. Testimony of Isabel Van Slyke, Book 3, p. 59; Corwin Statement, May 1935, p. 14.

29. On the "peace strike," see *Targum*, April 13, 1935.

30. *Campus News*, April 13, 1935. The letter was published anonymously, but for the names of the seven students who signed it, see Box 3, f., "Campus News." The main author of the letter was Theresa Kunst. She described her family as pro-Hitler. She was president of the N.J.C. League of Women Voters and a leader of the N.J.C. students who acted in behalf of Bergel. See Kunst's Testimony, Book 3, pp. 23ff. There had been some disagreement among the students who had taken up Bergel's cause over whether a petition or a letter to *Campus News* would be the more effective tactic to employ. They finally decided to write this letter. Bergel's testimony, Book 7, pp. 58–59.

31. *Campus News*, April 13, 1935. This was the final issue under the editorship of Frances Williams. She was succeeded by Marion Short.

32. Corwin Statement, May 1935, p. 14.

5. THE CRISIS

1. *Campus News*, April 24, 1935; May 1, 1935. For the identities of "Another Interested Group" and others who sent letters to *Campus News*, see Box 3, f., "Campus News-Letters to the Editor." Mrs. Hauptmann taught fifteen hours weekly for a salary of $1,080 in 1934–1935.

Between the academic years 1931–1932 and 1934–1935, enrollments in all language departments declined. German enrollments declined by 23.2 percent. Enrollments in French courses fell by 23.4 percent over the same period. The French Department had seven full-time faculty in 1932–1933, and in 1934–1935 there were five full-time and one part-time instructors. The decline in Spanish enrollments was 12.3 percent. Overall the college enrollment dropped by 15 percent. See data in Bergel Personnel File, 11, Douglass College Archives.

2. Meder Statement, 1935, pp. 9–10; Testimony of Frances Williams and Marion Short, *Daily Home News*, May 23, 1935. After the accusatory letter from

the "Group of German Students" appeared, Meder sent for Miss Short and told her that she had exercised "very poor editorial judgment," because some of the allegations appeared to him to be libelous. Short, however, refused to budge.

3. Meder Statement, 1935, p. 10; Testimony of Marjorie Fricke and Barbara Easton, *Daily Home News*, May 31, 1935.

4. "Seventy German Students," *Campus News*, May 8, 1935.

5. "Nine Alumnae," *ibid.*, May 8, 1935.

6. For the original of the petition, see Box 2, f. 8, "Bergel Exhibits." The document was attested to by Theresa Kunst under the date of May 20, 1935.

7. See Edna Newby to Meder, July 10, 1935, Box 1, f., "Committee Correspondence and Miscellaneous Records." Newby was a member of N.J.C.'s administrative staff.

8. "Trustees Committee Report," p. 37. The five-page pamphlet was published in Berlin by the Vereinigung Carl Schurz (Carl Schurz Association). Campbell, a medical doctor and a resident of New York, had been active since 1900 in several eugenics organizations. For the pamphlet, see Box 2, f. 7, "Bergel Exhibits." For Campbell's correspondence with Rolf Hoffmann of the Foreign Press Department of the Nazi Party, see "Records of the National Socialist Party, T-81, Roll 26, Frames 23056-61, National Archives, Alexandria, Va.

9. The Campbell pamphlet figured prominently in the hearing conducted by the Trustees' Special Committee. See Bergel's testimony, Book 1, pp. 30–33; Book 8, pp. 32–81. Hauptmann's testimony in *New York Herald-Tribune*, May 28, 1935, and *Daily Home News*, June 13, 1935; Corwin Statement, 1935, pp. 14–15. The *Daily Home News* did not print any story about the incident.

10. Bergel to Toolan, April 18, 1935, Box 2, f. 10, "Bergel Exhibits"; Toolan to Clothier, April 25, 1935, and Clothier to Toolan, April 29, 1935, Box 2, f. 12, "Committee Hearings, Exhibits, Committee Exhibits"; Bergel's testimony, Book 7, pp. 55–57, Book 8, pp. 353–354. It is possible that Bergel had been encouraged to bring his problem to the attention of public officials by Dr. Albert B. Meredith, the educational advisor to the Board of Regents. Meredith was a Cranford neighbor of the Bergels, and he had his own grievances against the University. He developed a close relationship with Bergel, attended most of the hearings, and was instrumental in helping Bergel secure a teaching position at Queens College in 1938. See, Bergel Interview, November 13, 1985, pp. 14–15, 39.

11. Bergel to Elliot, April 26, 1935, Box 2, f. 10, "Bergel Exhibits"; Bergel's testimony, Book 8, pp. 239, 354.

12. Clothier to Rafferty, May 6, 1935; Rafferty to Clothier, May 13, 1935, Box 4, f., "State of New Jersey." In his letter to Rafferty, and in his other letters regarding the controversy, Clothier always pointed to the two refugees in the Music Department as evidence of the lack of anti-Semitism at N.J.C.

13. Clothier to M. C. Phillips, April 30, 1935, Box 2, f. 4, "Bergel Exhibits"; Bergel Statement, May, 1935, p. 2.

14. Clothier Statement, July 1935, #2, p. 4.

15. Schmidt, *Douglass College*, p. 117; *Campus News*, March 9, 16, 1935;

Hauptmann Statement, 1935, p. 12; Hauptmann testimony, *Daily Home News,* May 28, 1935.

16. *Daily Home News,* May 3, 8, 1985.

17. Silver Interview, November 27, 1985.

18. *Ibid.,* Clothier Statement, May 1935, p. 2.

19. Clothier Statement, July 1935, #2, p. 4; Clothier Memo, undated, "Dr. Bergel Engaged as Instructor in German Department," Box 4, f., "Robert C. Clothier"; Bergel's testimony, Book 7, p. 67.

20. The main source for this important conversation is Bergel. See Bergel's testimony, Book 7, pp. 67–74, 81–82. There is no indication that Clothier prepared any memorandum of the meeting, which was also attended by A. S. Johnson, University Comptroller. According to Clothier, Bergel charged that "his failure to receive reappointment was due to his failure to agree with Prof. Hauptmann in his pro-Nazi sympathies." Clothier told Bergel that his coming to meet with him "did not alter the fact that his reappointment expires on June 30, 1935, but that if he cared to present a statement, I would be glad to have it considered." Clothier Statement, May 1935, p. 2.

21. Clothier Statement, July 1935, #2, p. 5; Ernest Little to C. R. Woodward, May 31, 1935, Box 4, f., "State of New Jersey"; *Newark Evening News,* May 20, 1935.

22. The issue with the geology professor was one of total incompatibility. For details on the case, see J. E. Ashmead Papers, 108–110, "Correspondence, 1935," and Trustee Papers, January 11, 1936. Clothier referred specifically to this case in a letter to Phillip M. Brett, May 11, 1935, Box 4, f., "Robert C. Clothier." There were similar proceedings in 1933 in a case that involved a clash between the Dean of the College of Agriculture and the Director of Extension. Whether Clothier first considered having a faculty panel hear the case, as Bergel reported, seems doubtful. Bergel's testimony, Book 7, pp. 74–75.

23. Silver did not recall how he communicated with the ACLU. As he remembered it, "somebody got on the phone." Silver Interview, November 27, 1985; Bergel's testimony, Book 8, pp. 358–362.

24. For information on the ACLU's Academic Freedom Committee, see David E. Bunting, *Liberty and Learning: The Activities of the American Civil Liberties Union in Behalf of Freedom of Education* (Washington, D.C., 1942). The archives of the ACLU are in the Seeley-Mudd Library at Princeton University. For a useful guide, see Alex Baskin, *The American Civil Liberties Union Papers: A Guide to the Records* (Stony Brook, N.Y., 1971). Most of the documents related to the Bergel case are in the volume labeled "1935–844, State Correspondence, New Jersey," but some useful items can be found in volumes 1935–762 and 1935–821. For the May 10 meeting, see Minutes, Committee on Academic Freedom, May 10, 1935, ACLU File, Rutgers University Archives; Bergel's testimony, Book 8, pp. 359–362. Evidently Bergel gave the committee a copy of the statement he had prepared for Harry S. Feller.

25. L. B. Milner to Clothier, May 11, 1935, ACLU File, Rutgers University

Archives. The threatened protest against the appropriations bill was a matter of some concern. Despite the adverse publicity that the University was getting in this period, the state appropriation for 1935–1936 provided an increase of $100,000 over the previous year. The Appropriation Act was approved on June 7, 1935. Ch. 239, *Laws of New Jersey*, 1935.

26. Telegram, Clothier to L. B. Milner, May 12, 1935, ACLU File, Rutgers University Archives.

27. A. J. Isserman to L. B. Milner, May 15, 1935, in *ibid.* Isserman was the most active person in the New Jersey ACLU. He became a member of the national board of the ACLU but resigned in 1940 as a consequence of the ACLU's decision to expel Communists from membership on the board. In 1949 he was one of five lawyers who defended Communist Party leaders prosecuted under the Smith Act. See Stanley I. Kutler, *The American Inquisition: Justice and Injustice in the Cold War* (New York, 1982), pp. 155–171. Clothier said later that the ACLU representatives "conceded that the letter which the [ACLU] had written . . . [him] was premature and unfortunate and apologized for it." See, Clothier Statement, July 1935, #2, pp. 5–6.

28. On Woltman, see *Who Was Who*, V, 1969–1973, p. 795; obituary in New York *Times*, March 6, 1970; "Academic Freedom in Pittsburgh," *New Republic*, May 22, 1929, pp. 21–22. Silver was under the impression that Clothier had been involved in Woltman's firing and that Woltman would therefore have a personal interest in the Rutgers case. In fact, Clothier did not assume his post as Dean of Men at Pittsburgh until after Woltman had departed. Silver Interview, November 27, 1985.

29. For Bergel's account of his communication with Woltman, see Bergel's testimony, Book 8, pp. 362–364.

30. *Ibid.*, pp. 364–365. The *New York Times, New York Herald-Tribune, Newark Evening News*, and *Daily Home News* all carried stories on May 16. On Birmingham see Bergel Interview, November 13, 1985, pp. 3–5, 13–14. Birmingham was a shadowy figure. He had once been a New York policeman, but he was dismissed from the force in 1921 for secretly holding down a second job. His firing made the newspapers, because the man he worked for was a suspected labor racketeer. (See *New York Times*, December 30, 1920; January 19, 1921.) Sometime in the 1930s Birmingham joined the staff of the McCormack-Dickstein Committee, the forerunner of the House Un-American Activities Committee. By 1938 he was listed as HUAC's chief investigator. (*New York Times*, September 16, 1938.) In his 1985 interview Bergel claimed that Birmingham appeared at his home after the hearings ended and gave him several hundred dollars, apparently from HUAC funds. Why Birmingham did this—if Bergel's recollection is accurate—is not at all clear.

31. Early drafts of Clothier's statements can be found in Box 4, f., "Robert C. Clothier." See also, Box 1, f., "Committee Correspondence and Miscellaneous Records," for other statements. At this time Clothier anticipated a brief hearing. "We hope to complete our investigation during the afternoon and to continue with

an evening session only if necessary," he wrote to J. Edward Ashmead, May 15, 1935, Box 1, f., "Committee Correspondence and Miscellaneous Records."

32. Clothier to J. Edward Ashmead, May 19, 1935, in *ibid.*, Box 1, f., "Communications to Committee—Resolutions of Organizations."

33. Clothier to Bergel, May 11, 1935, Box 2, f. 6, "Bergel Exhibits."

34. See Bergel to Clothier, May 13, 1935, Box 4, f., "Bergel and Counsel"; Clothier to Bergel, May 14, 1935, Box 2, f. 6. "Bergel Exhibits"; and Bergel to J. Edward Ashmead, May 18, 1935, Box 2, f. 6, "Bergel Exhibits." By this date, Bergel had conferred with A. J. Isserman of the ACLU. The ACLU had arranged for Frederick L. Redefer, executive secretary of the Progressive Education Association, to attend the hearing as its representative. William Newcorn, a lawyer from Plainfield, New Jersey, was provided for Bergel by "some of the Jewish organizations" interested in his cause, but he proved to be "absolutely useless" and was soon replaced. Newcorn was one of the three attorneys, led by Judge Siegler, who filed the brief with the Board of Regents in 1931 on discrimination against Jews at Rutgers. See L. B. Milner in Memorandum to Charles C. Weber, May 24, 1935, ACLU File, Rutgers University Archives.

35. Clothier Statement, July, 1935, #2, p. 2. For the successive drafts, see Box 4, f., "Robert C. Clothier."

36. Clothier expressed the same sentiments in *Annual Report of the President . . . 1934–1935*, p. 9. Bergel was one of four instructors at N.J.C. who were "not recommended for promotion" that year. Two of the others were in the Chemistry Department and the third was in the Psychology Department. See Dean Corwin to A. S. Johnson, Comptroller, July 9, 1935, Box 4, f., "Robert C. Clothier."

37. *Campus News*, June 1, 1935; *Targum*, June 8, 1935.

38. See, Box 1, f., "Communications to Committee—Submitting Evidence."

6. THE HEARINGS

1. See, "Above All Else, A Rutgers Man," *Rutgers Alumni Monthly*, December 1936, p. 4. Mrs. Lippincott, the only woman on the committee, was there to represent the interests of N.J.C. A graduate of Northwestern University, she was the first female member of the Camden Board of Education and a long-time advocate of woman's suffrage and world disarmament. While Lippincott asked very few questions during the hearings, she did serve as the committee secretary, taking detailed handwritten notes of the proceedings.

2. Clothier invited Meredith and Pesin to attend the hearings. Meredith, who acted as the liaison between the University and the Board of Regents, knew Bergel personally. Pesin, a powerful spokesman for Jewish interests in New Jersey, played a key role in the writing and adoption of the state's "Anti-Nazi Law." The biographical information on Sidney Kaplan was provided to our committee by Alice Yaeger Kaplan, Mr. Kaplan's daughter. Mr. Kaplan was actually Bergel's third attorney of the hearings. The first two—William Newcorn and C. D. Williams—dropped out after a couple of sessions.

3. Tauber is something of a mystery man. He lived in Jersey City and had a

law office at 21 West Street in Manhattan. According to the U.S. State Department's Index Files (Diplomatic Branch of National Archives), Tauber represented German companies (like Adolff Bobbin) that wanted to import their goods to America, as well as a number of German immigrants who had visa problems. Tauber's name also appeared in a document published by the House Un-American Activities Committee. The document, called "The Organization of German Industry in America After the War," was supposedly found in the files of a German-American businessman with close ties to the Nazi government. It stated, in part: ". . . there should be affiliated with the German Board of Trade the office of a customs attorney, for which position Mr. Fred G. Tauber has been proposed." The document did not say whether Tauber had agreed to take the position or whether, in fact, he knew anything about it. See Special Committee on Un-American Activities, *Investigation of Un-American Propaganda in the United States*, Appendix, part two, pp. 1104–1105, 1941.

4. A copy of the ACLU's report on the hearings is in Box 4, f., "American Civil Liberties Union." The quote appears on page 5.

5. Bergel Statement, May 1935, Box 2, f., "Committee Hearings, Exhibits, Bergel Exhibits, 23 and Unnumbered Documents." Bergel's "personal observation" about Hauptmann's pro-Nazi classroom harangue can be found in Bergel Testimony, Book 1, p. 35.

6. *Daily Home News*, May 22, 1935.

7. Shirley Smith "To the Special Committee of the Board of Trustees," May 19, 1935, Box 1, f., "Committee Hearing— Witnesses," 1 of 2.

8. See, *Daily Home News*, May 22, 1935; Van Dorn Testimony, Book 2, pp. 3–4, 21–22.

9. *Daily Home News*, May 22, 1935.

10. The witness who charged that Hauptmann had fired a book at her head was named Ethel Greenwald. Her testimony was disputed by several of her classmates. See *Daily Home News*, May 22, June 22, 1935. The witness who told the *Schweinehund* story was Ruth Wagner. Miss Wagner gave some of the most perplexing testimony of the hearings. She was Jewish and had taken several of Hauptmann's courses. Hauptmann had hired her to teach his classes during his leave of absence in Marburg. Miss Wagner had once considered Hauptmann a close friend. She had invited the Hauptmanns to her home, and her father had become Hauptmann's dentist. When Hauptmann returned home from his leave in Germany, however, Miss Wagner wanted nothing to do with him. She had changed her mind about Hitler's regime and was now anti-Nazi. How this transformation occurred is not known. Under stiff questioning, Miss Wagner admitted that she had met Mr. Bergel almost daily on the commuter train to New Brunswick during the months she had worked in the German Department. She also admitted that her conversations with Bergel had covered Hauptmann's "connection" with Germany. The trustees concluded that Miss Wagner's "whole testimony was so in conflict with the testimony of all other witnesses in the case that [we are] constrained to put no reliance on it." For Wagner's testimony, see, Book 5, pp. 1–57.

11. Atwood Testimony, Book 4, pp. 32, 34, 36, 41, 58, 68.

12. For testimony by Bergel's student witnesses about Hauptmann's alleged anti-Semitism, see remarks by Esther Weiss (May 22, 1935) and Ernestine Hanauer (July 6, 1935) in *Daily Home News*. Student witnesses for Bergel who disputed this contention include Isabell Shackel (May 22, 1935), Sylvia Silverman (May 22, 1935), Dorothy Venook (May 23, 1935), and Helen Lounsbury (May 25, 1935), in *ibid.*

13. Paul Freund to Margaret Corwin, (n.d.), Friedrich Hauptmann Personnel File, Douglass College Archives. The letter was probably written in February 1941 after Hauptmann had fled to Germany. Freund was replying to a letter written to him by Dean Corwin, dated January 30, 1941. What makes the letter so interesting (and genuine) is that Hauptmann apparently owed Freund money, which Freund was now trying to collect. Still, Freund remembered him fondly. For other letters relating to Hauptmann's fair treatment of Jews, see especially Edith Brauns to J. Edward Ashmead, May 28, 1935; Dorothy Geismar to J. Edward Ashmead, June 20, 1935; both in Box 1, f., "Communications to Committee—Submitting Evidence, Requests to Appear."

14. Hauptmann Statement, May, 1935, Box 2, f., "Committee Hearings—Exhibits, Hauptmann Exhibits."

15. *Ibid.*

16. *Ibid.*

17. *Ibid.*

18. Final Report, p. 11, copy in Box 5, f., "Final Report."

19. *Daily Home News*, June 7, 1935.

20. *New York Herald-Tribune*, May 28, 1935.

21. *Daily Home News*, June 15, 1935; *New York Herald-Tribune*, June 15, 1935.

22. *Daily Home News*, June 19, 1935. Jordan hinted at Bergel's radical views by saying he would "take Dr. Bergel's word" that he was not a Communist. Marga Holzmann, wife of Albert Holzmann, chairman of the Rutgers German Department, went a step further. She testified that Bergel was a "communist," a "socialist," and a "radical." Chairman Ashmead tried to focus her comments. "Do you think he is anti-democratic?" he asked. "Yes, perhaps that's better," she replied. There was, of course, not a shred of evidence for these malicious allegations. See New Brunswick *Sunday Times*, June 16, 1935.

23. *Daily Home News*, June 19, 1935.

24. *Ibid.*, June 16, 22, 1935.

25. *Ibid.*, June 16, 21, 22, 1935.

26. *Ibid.*, May 21, 1935.

27. Dorothy Geismar to J. Edward Ashmead, June 20, 1935, Box 1, f., "Communications to Committee—Submitting Evidence, Requests to Appear," 1 of 4.

28. Sidney J. Kaplan, "Confidential to the Committee," June 21, 1935, Box 4, f., "Bergel, Lienhard and Counsel."

29. Lucille Milner to J. Edward Ashmead, June 26, 1935, ACLU File, Rutgers University Archives.

30. Bergel's testimony, Book 7, p. 99.

31. *Ibid.*, p. 12.

32. *Ibid.*, p. 147–148.

33. *Ibid.*, pp. 134, 139–140.

34. Ruth Koester to Clothier, June 10, 1935; Dorothy Geismar to Ashmead, June 20, 1935, both in Box 1, f., "Communications to the Committee—Submitting Evidence, Requests to Appear," 1 of 4.

35. Bergel's Testimony, Book 7, p. 151.

36. *Ibid.*, p. 152.

37. *Daily Home News*, July 18, 1935. The statements of Corwin and Meder can be found in Box 4, f., "Administration—Statements by Officials." At another point in his statement, Meder said that "a lack of harmony in the department was feared, due to Mrs. Bergel's somewhat irritating and insistant personality."

38. *Daily Home News*, July 20, 1935.

39. *Ibid.*, July 24, 1935.

40. *Ibid.*

41. Final Report, p. 3.

42. *Ibid.*, pp. 10–11, 29.

43. *Ibid.*, pp. 34–38.

44. *Ibid.*, pp. 19–21.

45. *Ibid.*, p. 21.

7. THE AFTERMATH

1. Clothier to the Hauptmanns, August 17, 1935, Box 5, f., "Distribution, Opinions." 1 of 3.

2. See, Charles Reed to Clothier, August 22, 1935; Thomas Greene to Clothier, August 20, 1935; John Tinsley to Clothier, August 22, 1935, all in *ibid;* Earl R. Silvers to J. Edward Ashmead, August 30, 1935; Cyril J. McCauley to John W. Mettler, December 7, 1935, both in J. E. Ashmead Papers, 108–110; August Heckscher to Clothier, September 27, 1935, Trustee Papers.

3. T. A. Bisson to Clothier, August 28, 1935; Sylvia Dannett to Clothier, August 20, 1935, both in Box 5, f., "Distributions, Opinions," 3 of 3. Clothier was upset by Bisson's letter. He wrote to Earl Silvers, the director of Alumni Relations: "Please see the attached letter from Mr. T. A. Bisson, one of our alumni. Can you tell me anything about him?" Silvers sent Clothier a short biographical sketch of Bisson. He described Bisson, a specialist in Asian affairs, as one of Rutgers' most brilliant graduates. See Clothier to Silvers and Silvers' reply, September 14, 1934, *ibid.*

4. *New Brunswick Daily Home News*, August 20, 1935; *Jersey Journal,* as quoted in the *Daily Home News*, August 3, 1935.

5. *Deutscher Weckruf and Beobachter*, August 30, 1935; *Neue Volks-Zeitung*, November 2, 1935; *Staatszeitung und Herold*, August 20, 1935.

6. *Daily Home News*, August 20, 22; September 5, 7, 8, 1935.

7. A copy of the ACLU's Report is in Box 4, f., "American Civil Liberties Union."

8. *Daily Home News*, September 12, 1935.

9. Ellen Donahue to Roger Baldwin, October 26, 1935, in ACLU File.

10. Alan Silver to ACLU's Committee on Academic Freedom, October 12, 1935; Baldwin to Silver, October 16, 1935, both in *ibid.*

11. Two points should be made here. First, the AAUP had endorsed a "statement" on academic freedom and tenure drawn up by the American Council on Education in 1925. However, the statement had been approved by only a handful of universities as of 1940, and Rutgers was not one of them. Second, the AAUP was run from the top down in virtually every area. Local chapters had little influence on national policy. And, as noted, national AAUP officers were extremely cautious when it came to academic freedom cases—a policy that would continue into the McCarthy era. See, especially, Walter Metzger, *The Development of Academic Freedom in the United States* (New York, 1955); and Ellen Schrecker, *No Ivory Tower: McCarthyism and the Universities* (New York, 1986).

12. See, *AAUP Bulletin*, January 1935, p. 72.

13. Bergel to Ralph E. Turner, May 28, 1935; J.M.M. (Mr. Mayer, the treasurer) to W.C.C. (Mr. Cook, the general secretary), June 8, 1935; both in the AAUP File, Rutgers University Archives.

14. H.W.T. to W.W.C., September 18, 1935; J.M.M. to W.W.C., September 19, 1935; both in *ibid.*

15. Bergel to Silver, October 19, 1935; Milner to W. W. Cook, November 15, 1935; both in ACLU File.

16. H. W. Tyler to Milner, November 23, 1935; Milner to Tyler, December 5, 1935, both in *ibid.*

17. Tyler to Milner, December 6, 1935, in *ibid.*

18. Corwin to Jordan, September 13, 1985, Jordan Personnel File, Douglass College Archives.

19. Corwin to F. Hauptmann, November 26, 1935, F. Hauptmann Personnel File, Douglass College Archives.

20. Silver to Milner, September 23, 1935, in ACLU File.

21. Interview with Marion Short, May 23, 1986.

22. Donahue, "Memo," November 5, 1935; Donahue to Milner, September 23, 1935; both in ACLU File.

23. See *Daily Home News*, September 20, 1935; New Brunswick *Sunday Times*, September 15, 1935. The notes for Corwin, dated November 3, 1935, are in Bergel's Personnel File. A week after this meeting, the secretary of the N.J.C. Alumnae Association sent the following letter to all local club presidents: "A small group of alumnae . . . has organized to agitate for the reinstatement of Pro-

fessor Lienhard Bergel. . . . [We] wish to call attention . . . to the fact that this movement is in no way connected with your Association. The Executive Board has confidence in the decision of the trustees of the University and feels that an endeavor to reopen this case can bring nothing but harm to our College." See Mrs. John Moxon to Corwin, November 11, 1935; Moxon to Chapter Presidents, November 11, 1935; both in Bergel's Personnel File.

24. *New Brunswick Sunday times*, December 8, 1935.

25. Interview with Lienhard Bergel, November 13, 1985.

26. Sylvia Bergel to David M. Oshinsky, May 16, 1986, copy in the Committee File.

27. Bergel to Donahue, October 9, 1935; Donahue, "Memo," November 5, 1935; both in ACLU File. See also *Daily Home News*, February 26, 1936.

28. F. B. Robinson to Clothier, April 25, 1936, Bergel Personnel File, Douglass College Archives.

29. R.C.C., "Memorandum in re letter from President Frederick B. Robinson," April 29, 1936, in *ibid.*

30. George Van Santvoord to Head of the German Department, May 29, 1936, in *ibid.*

31. Corwin to Van Santvoord, June 1, 1936, in *ibid.*

32. Sylvia Bergel to David M. Oshinsky, May 16, 1986, copy in the committee's possession.

33. Hauptmann to Clothier, December 3, 1935, F. Hauptmann Personnel File, Douglass College Archives.

34. Interview with Albert Meder, December 10, 1985, Rutgers University Archives.

35. Corwin, "Notes of Meeting With Professor Hauptmann," January 1936, F. Hauptmann Personnel File, Douglass College Archives.

36. See *Daily Home News,* July 10, 1935.

37. Richard Segoine to J. Edward Ashmead, August 21, 1936, Ashmead Papers, 108–102, Rutgers University Archives.

38. E.R.S., "Above All Else—A Rutgers Man," *Rutgers Alumni Monthly,* December, 1936.

39. Corwin to Mettler, December 17, 1937; Mettler to Corwin, December 21, 1937; both in F. Hauptmann Personnel File. Mettler loaned Hauptmann approximately $3,000.

40. Mettler to Corwin, December 21, 1937.

8. THE COVER-UP

1. Dean Corwin to President Clothier, July 8, 1937; A. S. Johnson to Clothier ("Inter-Department Communication, Re Hauptmann"), July 9, 1937; both in Friedrich Hauptmann Personnel File, Douglass College Archives.

2. Corwin to President Ada Comstock, October 13, 1937, Werner Hollmann Personnel File, Douglass College Archives.

3. Comstock to Corwin, October 15, 1937, in *ibid.*

4. At the time of his hiring in 1937, Hollmann was working on a temporary basis at Finch Junior College in New York City. When Hollmann came to N.J.C., Corwin recommended Mrs. Hauptmann as his replacement at Finch. It is interesting to note that Corwin warmly recommended Mrs. Hauptmann and claimed (rather dubiously) that "her teaching has been excellent." Mrs. Hauptmann got the job. See, especially, Dean Corwin to Jessica Cosgrove, November 1, 1937, in F. Hauptmann Personnel File, Douglass College Archives.

5. The information on Hauptmann's citizenship comes from Friedrich Hauptmann FBI File, October 30, 1939, 65-1499-4, p. 9, Committee Files, Rutgers University Archives.

6. For Hauptmann's claim about serving the "cultural-political interests of the Reich," see Hauptmann Personnel File, BA R51/10036, Nazi Document Center, Coblenz, Germany. For the Hauptmann's many trips to Germany with their children, or to visit their children, see Friedrich Hauptmann FBI File, May 26, 1942, 65-1499-28; August 11, 1943, 65-1499-38, pp. 1–3.

7. Interview with Emil Jordan, February 26, 1986, Rutgers University Archives.

8. *Ibid.*

9. Evidence of Hauptmann's indebtedness can be found in dozens of letters, documents, and notes contained in his personnel file. For information on his purchase of the beauty shop, see: Friedrich Hauptmann FBI File, January 18, 1941, 65-1499-15, p. 4; Dean Corwin to Alma Stursberg, March 18, 1941, F. Hauptmann Personnel File, Douglass College Archives.

10. A copy of Dean Corwin's notes of this meeting, dated October 1, 1940, can be found in Hauptmann's Personnel File. It is interesting to note that the Dean of Rutgers College had a similar meeting with Professor Holzmann. Corwin's notes begin: "M.T.C. talked with Hauptmann. Explained that it was at request of President Clothier—that Dean Marvin was talking with Professor H. at Rutgers."

11. Hauptmann to Clothier, November 12, 1940, copy in F. Hauptmann Personnel file. Dean Corwin had a different recollection of this meeting. She claimed that "Hauptmann himself did almost all of the talking," that he spoke freely about "conflicting loyalties," that she made no mention of "adherence to [an] 'English-American' point of view," and that she never brought up the issue of his resignation. See Corwin to Clothier, November 16, 1940, copy in F. Hauptmann Personnel File, Douglass College Archives.

12. See U.S. War Department, War Crimes Office, Judge Advocate General's Office, Interrogation of Friedrich J. Hauptmann by Gerald Coates, Investigator for the 7708 War Crimes Group, APO 407, October 21, 1947, copy in Rutgers University Archives. Hauptmann's answers to various questions during his interrogation were self-serving and inaccurate. His story about his wife, therefore, should be taken with a grain of salt.

13. Hauptmann to Clothier, November 12, 1940, copy in F. Hauptmann Personnel File, Douglass College Archives.

14. Corwin to Clothier, November 16, 1940, copy in *ibid.*

15. Corwin to Clothier, November 20, 1940, in *ibid.*

16. Corwin to Clothier, November 23, 1940, in *ibid.*

17. The staffer's handwritten note, dated November 18, 1940, is in Hauptmann's Personnel File. See also Clothier to Hauptmann, November 19, 1940, in *ibid.*

18. See Friedrich Hauptmann FBI File, January 22, 1941, 65-1499-16, pp. 1–2.

19. All of the creditor's inquiries can be found in Hauptmann's Personnel File.

20. See Corwin to Paul Freund, January 30, 1941, Hauptmann Personnel File; also F. Hauptmann FBI File, January 22, 1941, 65-1499-16, pp. 1–2.

21. Clothier to Hauptmann, May 2, 1941, F. Hauptmann Personnel File.

22. The allegations that Hauptmann "received considerable mail from foreign places," that he "made suspicious contacts" with German vessels, and that he observed U.S. Army maneuvers with "an unidentified woman doctor," all can be found in F. Hauptmann FBI File, October 30, 1939, 65-1499-4, pp. 1–6. The rumor that Hauptmann kept pictures of Fort Hancock (Staten Island) in a trunk can be found in his FBI File, January 18, 1941, 65-1499-15, p. 6.

23. For the mail cover on Hauptmann, see his FBI File, March 7, 1940, 65-1499-6, pp. 1–5; for the "heresay" about the pictures of Fort Hancock and the statement about the reasons for Hauptmann's visits to the German vessels, see his FBI File, January 18, 1941, 65-1499-15, pp. 4–6.

24. See *Army and Navy Register,* August 25, September 1, 1934; *Army and Navy Journal,* September 1, 8, 15, 1934; *Report of the Secretary of War to the President,* GPO: 1935, pp. 64–65.

25. See Lienhard Bergel FBI File, January 30, 1943, pp. 1–5. A copy of this interview can also be found in Hauptmann's FBI File, January 30, 1943, 65-1499-35. In Bergel's file, the names of Jordan and Schlimbach are not blacked out; in Hauptmann's file, they are.

26. Sig. von Tiedemann to German Consulate General New York, "Re: Dr. Friedrich Johannes Hauptmann," May 8, 1941, copy in F. Hauptmann's FBI File, 65-1499-40.

27. Dr. Maria Keipert of the Political Archives of the German Foreign Office has informed our committee that the relevant consular materials and correspondence regarding Friedrich Hauptmann have either been discarded or destroyed. However, the internal indices of the German Foreign Office do reveal that the Cultural Section maintained a file on Hauptmann, listing four separate entries relating to the Bergel-Hauptmann hearings. The file was part of a larger folder about the appointments of German lecturers and instructors at American Universities.

In the spring of 1986 our committee requested the FBI's "German Archives File," which consists of approximately 3,200 pages of consular documents. The first batch of material—several hundred pages—arrived in the summer of 1987, shortly before our manuscript went to press. This material makes no mention of Professor Hauptmann.

9. WORKING FOR THE NAZIS

1. The best version of Hauptmann's return to Germany is contained in a report of a conversation he had with Dr. Heinz Nitzscke, the Chief of the Foreign Section of the German Academy. See Hauptmann Personnel File, Bundesarchiv Koblenz (Archives of the Federal German Republic). Hereafter cited as BA R51/10036. Copies in Committee Files, Rutgers University Archives.

2. March 15, 1941, conversation with Dr. Nitzscke, BA R51/10036.

3. Hauptmann's membership in the National Socialist Party is documented by his membership file at the Berlin Document Center. His personnel file for the German Academy does not list this membership but does document the help he received from the Foreign Office and the *Auslandsorganisation* of the Nazi party. See BA R51/10036.

Placing Hauptmann in the German Academy was surely no accident. Hauptmann's patron there was Professor Matthias Schmitz. Hauptmann and Schmitz had known each other from their days in America. Schmitz, who taught briefly at Smith College in Massachusetts, had been the director of the German Information Library attached to the German Consulate in New York City. He was widely regarded as one of Germany's leading propagandists in America during the 1930s. Returning to Germany in 1941, he was appointed General Secretary of the German Academy two years later. Not surprisingly, Hauptmann viewed Schmitz (whom he described as "an old fighting comrade from the U.S.A.") as a real asset to his own professional advancement. Indeed, with the assistance of Schmitz and the gratitude of the Foreign Office, Hauptmann was in a fine position to launch a promising career in the service of the Third Reich.

4. For the history of Slovakia, its break with Czechoslovakia, and its subsequent status as a German satellite, see Yeshayahu Jelinek, *The Parish Republic: Hlinka's Slovak People's Party, 1939–1945* (New York, 1976), especially pp. 32–50; Joerg K. Hoensch, *Die Slovakei und Hitlers Ostpolitik: Hlinkas Slovakische Volkspartei zwischen Autonomie und Separation 1938/1939* (Cologne, 1965); Joseph A. Mikus, *Slovakia: A Political History, 1918–1950* (Milwaukee, 1963); and Eugen Steiner, *The Slovak Dilemma* (Cambridge, 1973).

Curiously, Hauptmann's appointment to his position in Bratislava was described incorrectly by the German-language newspaper of the puppet state, which labelled him a German exchange professor. This may have been done deliberately. See *Grenzbote*, August 26, 1941. Cited in U.S. National Archives, Washington, D.C. German Records microfilmed at Alexandria, Virginia. World War II Records, Division T-175, *Reichsfuehrer SS and Chief of the German Police, Heinrich Himmler*, Role 532, Frame 9,403,450. Hereafter cited in abbreviated form: T-175, R 532, Fr. 9,403,450.

5. For the evolution of the German Academy (*Deutsche Akademie zur wissenschaftlichen Erforschung und zur Pflege des Deutschtums*), see Irene H. Hardcastle, "The Deutsche Akademie, Munich, 1932–1945," unpublished manuscript, 1981, National Archives, Washington, D.C.; Hans-Adolf Jacobsen, ed., *Karl*

Haushofer, Leben und Werk, 2 vols., 1979; Donald Norton, "Karl Haushofer and the German Academy, 1925–1945," *Central Europe* 1, no. 1 (March 1968), pp. 80–99. Much of the documentation concerning this organization is available in microfilm at the U.S. National Archives. German Records Microfilmed at Alexandria, Virginia, World War II Records Division, under the heading T-82 Records of German Cultural Institutions, *Deutsche Akademie,* Rolls 1–22. In 1941 Joseph Goebbels celebrated the Academy's new status by predicting that it would play a part in "The Final Solution of the Jewish Question." For the Academy's own estimation of its progress during its fifteen-year history, see Deutsche Akademie Muenchen, *Die Wissenschaft im Lebenskampf des deutschen Volkes: Festschrift zum fuenfzehnjaehrigen Bestehen der Deutschen Akademie am 5. Mai 1940.*

6. A secret appendix to the agreement between the Foreign Office and the Propaganda Ministry, signed by Goebbels and Ribbentrop, indicated that cultural attaches should generally be appointed by the Propaganda Ministry, while the Foreign Office would endow them with diplomatic respectability. For this largely unknown and very unconventional pact ("Working Agreement between the Reich Foreign Ministry") marked secret and dated October 22, 1941, see T-120, Roll 1423, Serial 2934H, Frs. D 567, 356–357.

7. For background on Hauptmann's inherited administrative, financial, and personnel problems, see his letters to Dr. Heinz Nitzschke, November 11, 1941; January 9, 1942; July 9, 1942. They are in the files of the German Federal Archives at Koblenz, *Bundesarchiv Koblenz,* in four folders containing the history of the German Academy Office in Pressburg or Bratislava, bearing the title *Deutsche Akademie Pressburg* (R51/178–181). We are indebted to Professor Harold Poor of Rutgers University, who went to Koblenz and selected the most important documents from this collection. For simplicity's sake, these documents have been abbreviated to read BA R51 Bratislava Files; they bear their entry or diary number (*Tagebuch Nummer*). Thus, *Tagb. Nrs.* 41/445, 42/662, and 8782.

8. For a sampling of Hauptmann's perpetual demands, see his correspondence with Dr. Heinz Nitzscke, December 22, 1941, Tagb. Nrs. 41/584–585; May 12, 1942, 42/1117 and 1119; June 5, 1942, 42/1236. For his rivalry with the Italians, see his memorandum, February 5, 1942, 42/761, to Dr. Stolz of the Academy's Foreign Department in Munich.

9. For the progressive reduction in his teaching, see his successive reports: *Zweiter Bericht der Mittelstelle fuer die Monate November-Dezember 1941/Zweiter Bericht im Arbeitsjahr 1941/42,* dated January 15, 1942, Tgb. Nr. 42/687, as well as *Arbeitsbericht fuer Maerz-April 1942,* 42/1420, all in BA Bratislava Files.

10. For a list of Hauptmann's speeches and their exclusive focus on American subjects, see his report of October 23, 1942, to Dr. Nitzschke, Tgb. Nr. 42/1835, Bratislava Files. For a virtually identical listing of Hauptmann's speeches in 1942, see *Mitteilungen der Deutschen Akademie: Deutsche Kultur im Leben der Voelker,* 17, no. 2 (November 1942), p. 346.

11. For Hauptmann's National Socialist views, see his letter to Dr. Nitzschke,

May 11, 1942, Tgb. Nr. 42/1107, BA R51, Bratislava Files. For information about the acquisition of the Jewish home, see Hauptmann's letter of March 8, 1944, BA R51, Bratislava Files. Hauptmann's most extreme racial statements are contained in a nine-page report on the situation in Slovakia, presented at a conference in Munich held in February 1944. See T-82, R. 21, Frs. 211,714ff.

12. The cultural attache, Dr. Hans Snyckers, was much younger than Hauptmann. He lived in a luxurious villa, spent money lavishly, and belonged to the brown-shirted S.A., in which he held the lofty rank of *Obersturmbannfuehrer*. Snyckers was extremely ambitious. He hoped to increase his authority in Slovakia by diminishing Hauptmann's. In short order, Snyckers suspended Hauptmann's weekly conferences with the Ambassador and thwarted Hauptmann's various attempts to take over control of the Academic Exchange Service in Slovakia and the proposed German Information Library at Bratislava. Hauptmann was so angry— "slowly the bile is rising in my stomach," he said—that he travelled to Berlin to see his friend Matthias Schmitz at the Propaganda Ministry. Although Snyckers won these battles, he was eventually removed from his position for "incompetence." For Hauptmann's futile attempts to obtain these posts, see Hauptmann to Snyckers T-175, R. 532, Fr. 9,403,467–69; Hauptmann to Nitzscke, March 5, 6, 9, 1942, Tgb. No. 42/855, 862, 881. For Snyckers's dismissal, see, T-175, R. 517, Frs. 9,384,989–995.

13. Hauptmann to Abteilung Auslandslektorate, November 3, 1942, Tgb. Nr. 42/1901, BA R51 Bratislava Files; Mader to Dr. Nitzscke, Head of the German Academy's Foreign Section, July 19, 1943. BA, Mader Personnel File, R51/10074. See also Hauptmann to Nitzscke, August 5, 1943, Hauptmann Personnel File, BA R51/10036.

14. The charge that Hauptmann had negotiated with other ministries is both interesting and baffling. In 1945 two non-Nazi former Academy officials wrote a fourteen-page document about the Academy's illicit political activities. In it the officials accused Hauptmann and five others of dealing with "agencies" whose activities were criminal in nature. However, these officials did not level specific charges; indeed, they claimed that evidence of Hauptmann's guilt could not be found in the records of the German Academy. (See Thierfelder and von Zwiedeneck-Suedenhorst, "Die politische Taetigkeit der Deutschen Akademie," August 21, 1945, T-82, Roll 14, Frs. 203,058ff.) The agencies in question could not have been the Propaganda Ministry or the Foreign Office, because such dealings were mandatory. It is unlikely that Hauptmann had criminal connections with the SS or the SD. The voluminous files of these notorious organizations make no mention of any direct connection with him. Indeed, their reports about his battles with Cultural Attache Snyckers portray Hauptmann with detached amusement.

For the Academy's attempts to get Hauptmann a medal and a job in post-war Germany, see the correspondence of Dr. Stroedel from January 3, 1945 to March 19, 1945, T-82, Roll 5, Frs. 193,568–70; Roll 5, Frs. 193,560f.; Roll 18, Frs. 208,031 and 208,935.

For allegations that Hauptmann had failed to provide a proper accounting for some currency transfers from a special discretionary fund, see T-82, Roll 22, Frs. 212,288–296, especially Fr. 212,290.

15. See Stroedel's "Aktennotiz fuer den Herrn Generalsekretaer," March 5, 1945, T-82, Roll 18, Fr. 208,497f.

16. See Schmitz to Hauptmann, April, 1945, T-82, Roll 22, Fr. 212,489; Stroedel's "Tageschronik," April 22, 1945, T-82, Roll 22, Frs. 212,490f.; Direktor Heitzer's "Atktennotiz," June 9, 1945, and Hauptmann to German Academy in Munich, October 26, 1945, both in BA R51/10036, Hauptmann Personnel File.

17. In his letter to Professor Holzmann, Cap said that the photograph of Hauptmann showed him in elegant attire at a 1944 Christmas gala held by the German Academy in Bratislava. That photograph (actually dated Christmas 1943) is now located in the Prints and Photographs Division of the Library of Congress. (Item 3145, Deutsche Akademie, Pressburg.) See also *New Brunswick Sunday Times*, June 16, 1946.

The files described by Major Baldwin had nothing to do with Nazi agents. They were the personnel files of the Academy's foreign service staff. The so-called propaganda library consisted of six thousand volumes belonging to the Academy's foreign department. For an inventory of the contents of Schloss Hoech, see Stroedel's "Umquartierung der Abteilung Auslandslektorate nach Schloss Hoech," November 21, 1944, T-82, Roll 22, Frs. 212,530–33, as well as a separate accounting by the Bavarian Minister of Education, D. Hipp, to the American Occupation Forces, including confirmation by the O.S.S. and other intelligence agencies, June 27, 1945, T-82, Roll 22, Frs. 212,603f.

18. Irene H. Hardcastle, "The Deutsche Akademie, Munich, 1923–1945," unpublished manuscript, 1981, National Archives, Washington, D.C., pp. 569–570.

19. For reports of Hauptmann's numerous arrests, see U.S. War Department, War Crimes Office, Judge Advocate General's Office, File No. 100-1226; also United States Intelligence and Security Command, Fort Meade, Maryland, Friedrich J. Hauptmann File of Counter Intelligence Corps, 430th CIC Detachment, Land Salzburg Section, September 11, 1947, no. 860723286 and MSN 48454 S35F248. Copies are on file in the Rutgers University Archives.

20. See Lienhard Bergel to Chief of Operations, War Crimes, Civil Affairs Division, June 28, 1947; T. Vincent Quinn, Assistant Attorney General to Lieutenant Colonel Ray J. Laux, GSC, Army Civil Affairs Division, September 25, 1947, in U.S. War Department, War Crimes Office, Hauptmann File, 100-1226.

21. For the text of this six-page interrogation, see U.S. War Department, War Crimes Office, Hauptmann File, 100-1226. A copy is on file in the Rutgers University Archives.

22. We are indebted for material about Hauptmann's life in post-World War II Austria to Professor Fritz Fellner of the University of Salzburg and his assistants, Johann Kolmbauer and Michael Mooslechner, who provided a comprehensive report. Hereafter cited as Salzburg Report.

23. For Friedrich Hauptmann's attempts to return to America, see David Ross

to the President (sic), New Jersey College for Women, September 9, 1949; Margaret Corwin to Ross, September 13, 1949; both in Friedrich Hauptmann Personnel File, Douglass College Archives. For the loss of Hauptmann's citizenship, see his American Expeditionary Force, Displaced Persons Registration Record, quoted in the University of Salzburg Report. Mrs. Hauptmann applied for an immigration visa on October 4, 1949. She listed her occupation as housewife. According to her certificate of naturalization, she became an American citizen on December 8, 1955.

24. See University of Salzburg Report.

25. *Ibid.* This report includes a picture of the tombstone.

EPILOGUE

1. New Brunswick *Home News*, May 8, June 11, September 27, 1985.

2. Peter Parisi was denied tenure in the Rutgers English Department in the 1970s. In a conversation with David Oshinsky, chairman of the Bergel-Hauptmann Committee, Parisi complained that our Interim Report read like his own promotion report—the one that ended his chances for permanent employment at Rutgers.

3. *New Brunswick Home News*, December 19, 1986; January 9, 1987.

4. *Ibid.*, January 27, 1987.

5. *Ibid.*, April 19, 1987.

6. *Port Washington News* (L.I.), January 7, 1988.

7. *New Brunswick Home News*, December 16, 1987.

8. *New Brunswick Home News*, April 19, 1987.

A Note about the Sources

While researching the Bergel-Hauptmann case, our committee used many primary documents. The vast majority of them are now open for public review at the Rutgers University Library. The major exceptions are college personnel files of Lienhard Bergel, Friedrich and Marie Hauptmann, Emil Jordan, and other faculty members of that era. Because of university regulations, these files must remain closed to the public. Those interested in studying the available documents should first consult the *Guide to Sources Relating to The Bergel-Hauptmann Case*, prepared by Rutgers archivist Ruth Simmons and her staff. The *Guide* is on file in the Library's New Jersey Room.

The available documents include:

(1) The "Special Trustees Committee (1935) to Investigate the Charges of Lienhard Bergel." These five boxes contain the 1935 Trustees Report; transcripts of testimony taken at the 1935 hearings; exhibits from those hearings; communications to the trustees committee; correspondence from that committee; statements by witnesses before that committee; clippings from *Targum, Campus News*, the *New Brunswick Daily Home News*, and other newspapers; and various documents relating to the case.

(2) Papers of President Robert C. Clothier.

(3) Papers of J. Edward Ashmead, chairman of the Special Trustees Committee.

(4) Trustee Minutes and Papers.

(5) Douglass College Record Group, especially Records of the

Dean, Box 32, for statistics and enrollment figures during this period.

(6) Files of the 1985–86 Bergel-Hauptmann Committee. These files were gathered during our months of research. They include:

   (a) Transcripts of interviews with Lienhard Bergel, Emil Jordan, Alan Silver, and Albert Meder.

   (b) Copies of relevant documents from the ACLU Papers at Princeton University.

   (c) Copies of relevant documents from the AAUP Papers at the Association's headquarters in Washington, D.C.

   (d) Correspondence with Alan Silver.

   (e) Correspondence with Lienhard and Sylvia Bergel.

   (f) Copies of the FBI files of Friedrich Hauptmann and Lienhard Bergel, as well as parts of the FBI's "German Archives File."

   (g) Copies of the U.S. Immigration and Naturalization files relating to Friedrich and Marie Hauptmann.

   (h) Copies of German documents and microfilms relating to Friedrich Hauptmann's activities during World War II. This file contains material gathered from Bundesarchiv Koblenz (Archives of the Federal German Republic); the U.S. National Archives, World War II Records Division; the U.S. National Archives, Diplomatic Branch; the U.S. National Archives Records Center, Suitland, Maryland; and the Library of Congress, Prints and Photograph Division.

   (i) Copies of U.S. Army Intelligence files relating to the interrogation of Friedrich Hauptmann following World War II.

   (j) Copy of the University of Salzburg Report documenting the post-World War II activities of Friedrich J. Hauptmann.

Our committee also studied a number of newspapers, periodicals, dissertations, and books. They include:

NEWSPAPERS

Army and Navy Register, 1934
Campus News, 1932–1936.
Deutscher Weckruf und Beobachter, 1934–1937
Neue Volks-Zeitung, 1934–1937
Newark News, 1946
New Brunswick Home News, 1935–1937, 1946, 1985–1987
Newsday, 1985–1987
New Yorker Staatszeitung und Herold, 1934–1937
New York Times, 1921, 1924, 1935–1937, 1946, 1985–1987
New York World Telegram, 1935–1937
Targum, 1932–1936, 1985–1987
Toronto Globe and Mail, 1985–1987

PERIODICALS

"Above All Else, A Rutgers Man," *Rutgers Alumni Monthly,* December 1936.
"Academic Freedom in Pittsburgh," *The New Republic,* May 22, 1929.
Ashkensas, Bruce, "A Legacy of Hatred: The Records of a Nazi Organization in America," *Prologue,* 17 (Summer 1985).
Draper, Hal, "The Student Movement of the Thirties," in Rita Simon (ed.), *As We Saw the Thirties* (Urbana, Ill., 1967).
Jordan, Emil, and Alice Schlimbach, "The German House: A Successful Educational Experiment in Modern Language Teaching on a College Campus," *The Modern Language Journal,* XX (March 1936).
Luebke, Frederick, "The Germans," in John Higham (ed.), *Ethnic Leadership in America,* (Baltimore, 1978).
McMillan, Neil, "Pro-Nazi Sentiment in the United States, March 1933–March 1934," *Southern Quarterly,* 11 (October 1963).
Mitteilungen der Deutschen Akademie: Deutsche Kultur im Leben der Voelker, 1941–1943.
Norton, Donald, "Karl Haushauser and the German Academy, 1925–1945," *Central Europe,* 1 (March 1968).

DISSERTATIONS

Hardcastle, Irene, "The Deutsche Akademie, Munich, 1932–1945," 1981, copy on file at the National Archives, Washington, D.C. Hauptmann, Friedrich, "Eine wissenschaftliche Kritik des Standes des Deutschen Unterrichts an den High Schools und Colleges der Vereinigten Staaten," Marburg, 1937.

BOOKS

Baeumler, Ernst, *Politik und Erziehung* (Berlin, 1937).
Bracher, Karl, *The German Dictatorship* (New York, 1970).
Broun, Heywood and George Britt, *Christians Only: A Study of Prejudice* (New York, 1931).

Bunting, David, *Liberty and Learning: The Activities of the American Civil Liberties Union in Behalf of Freedom of Education* (Washington, D.C., 1942).

Diamond, Sander, *The Nazi Movement in the United States, 1924–1941* (Ithaca, N.Y., 1974).

Diggins, John, *Mussolini and Fascism: The View From America* (Princeton, N.J., 1972).

Goodman, Walter, *The Committee: The Extraordinary Career of The House Committee on Un-American Activities* (New York, 1968).

Hanfstaengl, Ernst, *Hitler: The Missing Years* (London, 1957).

Hoensch, Joerg, *Die Slovakei und Hitler's Ospolitik: Hlinka's Slovakische Volkspartei zwischen Autonomie und Separation, 1938–1939* (Cologne, 1965).

Jacobsen, Hans-Adolf (ed.), *Karl Haushofer, Leben und Werk*, 2 vols., (Berlin, 1979).

Jelinek, Yeshayahu, *The Parish Republic: Hlinka's Slovak People's Party, 1939–1945* (New York, 1976).

Kater, Michael, *Studentenschaft und Rechsradikalismus in Deutschland, 1918–1933* (Hamburg, 1975).

Koshar, Rudy, *Bourgeois Marburg, 1880–1935: Social Life, Local Politics, and Nazism* (Chapel Hill, N.C., 1987).

Krieck, Ernst, *Nationalpolitische Erziehung* (Osterwieck, 1933).

Kutler, Stanley, *The American Inquisition: Justice and Injustice in the Cold War* (New York, 1982).

Lipstadt, Deborah, *Beyond Belief: The American Press and the Coming of the Holocaust, 1933–1945* (New York, 1986).

McCormick, Richard, *Rutgers: A Bicentennial History* (New Brunswick, N.J., 1966).

McKale, Donald, *The Swastika Outside Germany* (Kent, Ohio, 1977).

Metzger, Walter (ed.), *The American Concept of Academic Freedom in Formation* (New York, 1977).

———, *The Development of Academic Freedom in the United States* (New York, 1955).

Mikus, Joseph, *Slovakia: A Political History: 1918–1950* (Milwaukee, 1963).

Schleunes, Karl, *The Twisted Road to Auschwitz: Nazi Policy Toward German Jews, 1933–1938* (Urbana, Ill., 1970).

Schmidt, George, *Douglass College: A History* (New Brunswick, 1968).

Schrecker, Ellen, *No Ivory Tower: McCarthyism and the Universities* (New York, 1986).

Silberman, Charles, *A Certain People: American Jews and their Lives Today* (New York, 1985).

Steinberg, Stephen, *Sabers and Brownshirts: The German Students' Path to National Socialism, 1918–1933* (Chicago, 1977).

Steiner, Eugen, *The Slovak Dilemma* (Cambridge, 1973).

Wechsler, James, *Revolt on the Campus* (New York, 1935).

Weinreich, Max, *Hitler's Professors: The Part of Scholarship in Germany's Crimes Against the Jewish People* (New York, 1946).

Index

American Association of University
Professors (AAUP), 4, 112, 127 n35,
140 n11; post-hearings activities,
78–79; on termination of instruc-
torships, 21

American Civil Liberties Union
(ACLU): charges against German
Department, 51; reaction to Ashmead Report, 77; stand on compromise at trustees hearings,
68–69; support of Bergel, 51

American Youth Congress, New Jersey
Division, 40

Anti-Nazi Law of 1935 (New Jersey),
39, 44, 131 n22

anti-Semitism, 16, 34–35, 46, 59–
60, 62, 65, 101–102

Army War Crimes Group, U.S., interrogation of Hauptmann, 105,
142 n12

Ashmead, J. Edward, 57

Ashmead Report, 72, 73, 74; accepted by trustees, 79; reaction to,
75–78

Baldwin, Roger, 77

Bergel, Lienhard, 22, 25, 26, 30, 31,
56, 78–79, 108; appointment to
German Department, 11, 124 n13;
assessed by colleagues, 13; attendance at faculty meetings, 25,
128 n8; charges against German
Department, 36–37, 59–60;

charges against Hauptmann, 1, 36,
47, 56, 58–59, 69, 96, 105,
126 n31, 134 n20; charges investi-
gated, 2; compared with Hauptmann, 12–13; compromise offered
at trustees hearings, 67–68; death,
111; discussion with Clothier, 50;
discussion of Nazism, 15; dismissal, 1, 19, 27, 42, 108; early
account of, 12; and the FBI, 82,
96; interviewed by *Campus News*,
14; Jewish student support for, 46;
joins NJC faculty, 12; later career,
84 n; letter in support of, 51; letters
of recommendation, 129 n19; meetings with Corwin, 28–29; national
attention for, 49; post-hearings activities, 81–83; protests against
dismissal of, 2; at Queens College,
2, 84; quoted in 1985, 5; reaction
to dismissal, 21; reappointment denied, 73; reasons for dismissal of,
19, 26–27, 29, 50, 112; in retirement, 5; testimony at trustees
hearings, 58–60, 69–71

Bergel, Sylvia (Cook), 3, 5, 19, 83;
on German Department, 28–29;
letter to Corwin (1934), 28–29;
letter to *Home News* (1985), 121 n3;
note to state legislators (1935), 39;
letter to Bloustein (1985), 5; married, 12

Birmingham, Stephen, 53, 57, 135 n30

Bisson, T. A., 139n3
Bloustein, Edward J.: appoints review panel, 4–5; defends university action, 109; refuses to reopen case, 3; on reopening case, 4
Braun, William A., 12; letter to Meder, 126n32; letter to Sylvia Bergel, 126n33
Brett, Philip M., 57
Burns, Edward M., 15

Campbell, Clarence G., 46; "A Foreign Visitor's Impressions of Germany," pamphlet, 46–47
Campus News: on Bergel's dismissal, 41–42; on campus peace strike, 40; interview with Bergel, 14; letters supporting Bergel in, 45–46
campus peace strike, 40, 41
Cap, Edward, 2, 24
Chaneles, Edward, 110, 110n
City College of New York, 83
Clark, Evalyn, 24
Clothier, Robert C., 27, 33, 34, 50, 54, 83, 86, 92, 94; account of, 37–38; baccalaureate address (1935), 55; criteria for judging teachers, 54–55; discussion with Bergel, 50; on freedom of speech, 55; investigative committee appointed by, 2; meeting with ACLU representatives, 52; objectives of 1935 inquiry, 53; refusal to reopen case (1946), 2; testimony at trustees hearings, 71–72
Committee for Academic Freedom (NJC), 81
Comstock, Ada, 89
Consumers' Research, letter to Corwin, 48
Corwin, Margaret Trumbull, 26, 27, 28–29, 33, 44, 86, 92, 93, 94, 126n28, 142n4; account of, 22–23; on Bergel's charges, 37; on

language teaching, 37; letter to Bergel (1934), 27; meeting with Hauptmann (1940), 91; meetings with Bergel (1934), 28–29; testimony at trustees hearings, 71

Daily Home News. See Home News, New Brunswick
Dickstein, Samuel, 24
Donahue, Ellen, 77, 78, 81
Douglass, Mabel Smith, 9, 23, 126n28
Douglass College (New Jersey College for Women), 1

Edelstein, Tilden, 4

Federal Bureau of Investigation (FBI), 82, 94, 96
Feller, Harry S., 34, 35, 37
"Foreign Visitor's Impressions of Germany," pamphlet, 46–47
Freund, Paul, 138n13
Friends of New Germany (FONG), 13–14, 24

German Academy (Deutsche Akademie), 99–100
German Department (NJC), 1, 9, 18–19, 28–29, 33, 130n13; charges of Nazi support in, 44; cuts required (1934), 42; defended, 45; development under Hauptmann, 10–11; in 1937, 88
German House (NJC), 11, 31, 36, 45, 62, 66, 67, 69

Hanfstaengl, Ernst "Putzi," 32
Hauptmann, Anna Marie, 30n, 80, 80n, 86, 89, 147n23; comes to U.S., 10; divorce, 106; leaves U.S. for Germany, 91, 93; returns to U.S. (1949), 106; as teaching assistant, 11

Hauptmann, Friedrich J., 5, 15, 16, 22, 25, 26; and anti-Semitism, 101–102; arrest (1947), 105–106; arrest and internment (1945–1946), 104–105; in Austria, 103; becomes head of German Department (NJC), 10; in Bratislava, Slovakia, 99–103, 146 n14; buys beauty parlor, 90; children, 89–90; compared with Bergel, 12–13; death, 106–107; defended, 45; disappearance, 2, 92–95, 98; discussion with Hanfstaengl, 32; dissertation, 32–33, 130 n7; early account of, 9–10; and Erna Zoller, 11; finances, 85–87, 90, 93–94; German House (NJC) support, 45; in Germany (1934–1935), 31–33; at Gettysburg College, 10, 123 n8; and Hans Snyckers, 146 n12; on Hitler, 17; joins German Department (NJC), 10; joins Nazi Party, 99; leave of absence, 31; letter of dismissal, 95; letter from Joseph Goebbels, 1; loyalty to Germany, 92; and Lutheran Church, 10, 123 n8; and Matthias Schmitz, 144 n3; meeting with Clothier (1935), 48; meetings with Corwin (1940), 91; post-hearings activities, U.S., 85–86; and question of espionage, 95–97; retirement offer, 92; return to Germany, 98; salary increase, 88; student witnesses for at trustees hearings, 66–67; testimony at trustees hearings, 63–65; U.S. citizenship of, 89
Heckscher, August, 75
Hickman, Emily, 33
Hoffman, Milton J., 16
Hollmann, Werner, 88–89, 142 n4
Holzmann, Albert, 14, 15, 17
Holzmann, Marga, 138 n22
Home News, New Brunswick: account of Bergel dismissal, 1; on Bergel's death, 111–112; conference with investigative committee (1985), 110–111; editorial stand (1987), 108, 109; editorials (1985), 3, 5; reaction to Ashmead Report, 76
Hotchkiss School, 84

Investigative Committee (1985): conference with *Home News*, 110–111; created, 6; interim report released, 108; questions raised, 6
Isserman, Abraham (A. J.), 52, 135 n27, 136 n34

Jewish students at NJC, 35
Johnson, A. S., 88
Jordan, Emil, 11, 33–34, 138 n22; account of, 27–28; in Germany, 90; *Kultur-Geographie von Deutschland*, 28; later account of, 128 n14; loans to Hauptmann, 90; on Nazism, 15; promotion, 28; testimony at trustees hearings, 66

Kaplan, Sidney J., 58, 72, 76, 136 n2
Keller, Nathaniel, 15–16
Kreutzer, Leonid, 13

Lassner, Oscar, 33
Lippincott, Miriam, 57, 136 n1
Loiseaux, C. E., 39
Loyalty Oath, New Jersey, 39

McCormack-Dickstein Committee, 39, 44
Mader, Julius, 102–103
Meder, Albert E., 26, 29; and *Campus News*, 44–45; conference with Hauptmann, 22; faculty promotion standards of, 18; meeting with Bergel, 19–20; testimony at trustees hearings, 71

Meredith, Albert B., 57, 133 n10, 136 n2
Mettler, John Wycoff, 57, 86–87
Metzger, Fraser, 49, 51
Milner, Lucille, 79

National Student League (NSL), 24, 49; local chapter organized, 40; reaction to Ashmead Report, 77
Nazism: American reaction to, 13–14; campus viewpoint of, 16–17, 33; charges of faculty support, 1, 44; discussion of, 15; Emil Jordan on, 15; opposition to, 14; student interest in, 14; and subversion in U.S., 24–25
New Brunswick Home News. See Home News, New Brunswick
Newcorn, William, 136 n34
New Jersey Board of Regents, 7
New Jersey College for Women (NJC), 1, 7; budgetary figures and salaries, 122 n3; created, 9; development, 9; educational philosophy (1932), 11; enrollment (1929–1934), 8; faculty (1933), 125 n26; faculty promotion standards, 18; language departments' enrollment (1931–1935), 132 n1
New Jersey College for Women Alumnae Association, 140 n23
New York World Telegram, Woltman article (1935), 53

Parisi, Peter, 1, 2, 108, 109, 111, 143 n2; article on Bergel dismissal, 1–2; on interim report, 109–110
peace strike (1935), 40, 41
Pesin, Samuel, 57, 76, 136 n2

Queens College, Bergel hired by, 84

Rafferty, John J., 47, 131 n22
Raven, John, 57

Redefer, Frederick L., 136 n34
Rudolfs, Willem, 24
Rutgers University: Bergel dismissal upheld by trustees, 2; committee on personnel procedures, 122 n2; enrollment (1929–1934), 8; and the Great Depression, 8; history before 1932, 7; nepotism rule, 80 n; personnel policies, 8; state appropriations (1935), 134 n25; salaries (1935), 8; three-year rule, 18, 26, 30 n, 127 n34

Schlimbach, Alice, 11, 31; testimony at trustees hearings, 65–66
Schmitz, Matthias, 144 n3

Short, Marion, 44–45, 132 n2
Siegler, Joseph, 34–35
Silver, Alan, 1, 50, 51, 77, 80, 80 n, 109, 110; criticism of interim report, 30 n, 108; and Frederick E. Woltman, 52; national attention brought to Bergel case by, 49; on NSL objectives, 40; public investigation demanded by, 49; on reopening Bergel case (1985), 3
Smith, Shirley: letter to trustees, 60; testimony at trustees hearings, 60
Snyckers, Hans, 146 n12
Special Trustees Committee (1935): membership, 57; report (*see* Ashmead Report). *See also* trustees hearings (1935)
student activism, 23, 39–40, 131 n24
Students League for Industrial Democracy (SLID), 24

Targum, 16, 23, 131 n24
Tauber, Fred G., 58, 72, 136 n3
three-year rule. *See* Rutgers University, three-year rule
Toolan, John E., 47

trustees hearings (1935): agreed upon, 52; Bergel's testimony, 58–60, 69–71; decision, 72–73; ground rules defined, 58; Hauptmann testimony, 63–65; length and scope, 57; objectives, 54; offer of compromise by Bergel, 67–68; post-hearings reaction, 75–78; records of, 124n14; redefined, 56; student testimony for Bergel, 61–62; student testimony for Hauptmann, 66–67; witnesses for Bergel, 60–62; witnesses for Hauptmann, 65–66. *See also* Special Trustees Committee (1935)

Van Dorn, Harold, 48; testimony at trustees hearings (1935), 61

Wagner, Ruth, 137n10
Waksman, Selman A., 38, 38n, 50
Woltman, Frederick E., *New York World Telegram* article, 53, 108

Zoller, Erna, 11–12